D0876816

...es You

And Other Expressions and Proverbs from Sy...

W/N

Also by Rebecca Joubin

Two Grandmothers from Baghdad:
And Other Memoirs of Monkith Saaid (2004)

Afsaneh, A Novel from Iran (2013)

The Politics of Love: Sexuality, Gender, and Marriage in
Syrian Television Drama (2013)

Your Mother-in-Law Loves You
and Other
Expressions and Proverbs
from Syria

حَماتِك بِتْحِبّك

Compiled by Rebecca Joubin

Illustrated by Etab Hreib

Ibex Publishers
Bethesda, Maryland

Your Mother-in-Law Loves You
and Other Epressions and Proverbs from Syria
Compiled by Rebecca Joubin
Illustrated by Etab Hreib

ISBN: 978-1-58814-132-3

Manufactured in the United States of America

The paper used in this book meets the minimum requirements of the American National Standard for Information Services—Permanence of Paper for Printed Library Materials, ANSI Z39.48–1984

Ibex Publishers strives to create books which are as complete and free of errors as possible. Please help us with future editions by reporting any errors or suggestions for improvement to the address below, or corrections@ibexpub.com

Ibex Publishers, Inc.
Post Office Box 30087
Bethesda, Maryland 20824
Telephone: 301–718–8188
Facsimile: 301–907–8707
www.ibexpublishers.com

Library of Congress Cataloging-in-Publication Data

Joubin, Rebecca, compiler.
Your mother-in-law loves you : a bilingual collection of expressions and proverbs from Syria / compiled by Rebecca Joubin ; illustrated by Etab Hreib.
pages   cm
1. Proverbs, Arabic—Syria.   2. Proverbs, Arabic—Translations into English.   3. Arabic language—Syria—Terms and phrases.   I. Hreib, Etab, illustrator.   II. Title.
PN6519.A7J68 2014
398.9'927095691—dc23
2014028651

For my daughter, Jana,

and to all my students,
who inspire me more than they can imagine

CONTENTS

INTRODUCTION

I traveled to Damascus in 2000 and 2001, resided there from 2002 until 2008, and then returned for fieldwork during the summers of 2010 and 2011. During this time in which I conducted research on Syrian culture, I collected expressions and proverbs I heard in casual conversation or when viewing Syrian television dramas and films. The continual use of proverbs and expressions in daily conversations and artistic production fascinated me.

I began teaching Arabic language and culture at Davidson College during the fall of 2009, and have introduced these proverbs to my students at all levels of language study. In the same way these proverbs mesmerized me when I first immersed myself in the language and culture of Syria, my students were captivated. As I began compiling these proverbs to teach in my own coursework, the project expanded. I soon realized that I had a wide selection of expressions and proverbs to share not only with my own students, but with others studying Arabic as well as Syrian language and culture.

I have divided these proverbs and expressions into thematic sections such as the body, food, animals, and colors. I also have sections on themes such as the homeland, work, experience, and forgiveness. Sometimes, a proverb can fit into two sections, but I have chosen to place it just in one section to avoid repeating the same proverb. Consider the following proverb, for example:

الرَسول شايِفْ بِعيونُه وسَتَرْ : الرَسولُ رأى بِعيونِهِ وَسَتَّرَ

The Prophet saw the sinner with his own eyes and protected him.

Don't gossip and judge others harshly.

In this case, I have placed this proverb in the section on gossip, because I felt it would stand out better there, than in the section on "eyes." Or, consider the following example:

الإرِد بِعَيْن إمَّه غَزال : القِردُ بِعَيْنِ أمَّه غَزالٌ

A monkey is a gazelle in his mother's eyes.

Beauty is in the eye of the beholder.

I have placed this proverb in the section on "eyes," in the first group of expressions and proverbs using body parts. There is no particular reason, but the fact that I wanted to avoid repeating it again in the section on animals.

It was my hope to show the universal nature of many of these proverbs. Thus, after the literal translation rather than spelling out its exact meaning, I have often written a similar proverb used in the Western context. For example:

إِذَا دَخَلْتَ إلى بَلَدِ عُورانٍ ضَعْ يَدَكَ عَلى عَيْنِكَ : إِذَا فَتِتْ عَبَلَدْ عُوران حُطْ إِيدَك عَعَيْنَكْ

If you enter a country where people have only one eye, cover one of your eyes.

When in Rome, do as the Romans do.

In the interest of those both teaching and learning Modern Standard Arabic, I have designated the left hand column for Modern Standard Arabic, which I have written in bold. To the right side is Syrian colloquial. There are cases when a proverb or word can only be stated in Modern Standard Arabic, and all those are placed in bold without a colloquial expression next to it. I have written both the literal translation and the contextual meaning in English of each proverb and expression for those interested to see the play on words. In case where the literal translation and contextual meaning are the same I have only written the definition once.

It is my hope that by compiling these proverbs, students of Arabic, as well as Syrian culture in particular, can gain a window into understanding the diversity of Syrian cultural expression. We can also see much contradiction and various perspectives on the roles of men, women, and children, serving as a reminder that we cannot essentialize Syrian culture. At the same time, we learn about universal values and esteemed attributes in Syrian culture such as hospitality, generosity, forgiveness, and humility.

I chose for the title: "*Hamatik ba-Tohebik*" (Your Mother-in-Law Loves You), since it has always been the first expression I introduce to my students and has always been one that sticks with them. "Your Mother-in-Law Loves You" means you have come right when we are about to eat or drink and we would love for you to join us. It signals an impromptu arrival and attests to the warmth shown toward guests.

Illustrations are by internationally-acclaimed Syrian watercolorist, Etab Hreib. In addition to drawing the illustrations for this book, these past years she has traveled to Davidson College several times to conduct art workshops with my students. I am most grateful for her generosity of spirit. Without the incredible support I have received from Davidson College, I could not have completed this book. The generous stipend I have received annually due to my Malcolm O. Partin Assistant Professorship, as well as a Dean Rusk summer grant, allowed me to travel to Damascus twice to conduct my research. During the spring of 2014, my talented research assistant Arielle Korman read the final draft of this book and provided incisive critique and invaluable suggestions.

At a time when Syria is constantly in the press, with images of bloodshed and violence essentializing Syrian culture, it is my hope that this illustrated book of Syrian proverbs, the first of its kind in the English language, will show another, more nuanced face of Syria. I am honored to dedicate this book to my daughter, Jana, and to all my students, who inspire me more than they can imagine.

— Rebecca Joubin

THE BODY

EARS

الأُذُنْ (آذان)

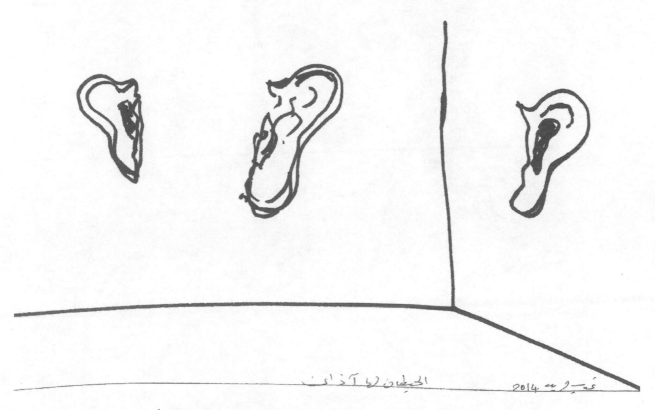

حيطانْ الحارَة إلون آذان كُبار : جِدارُ الحارَةِ لَها آذانٌ كَبيرةٌ

The walls of the neighborhood have big ears.

Walls have ears.

حُطْها حَلاة بإذنَك : ضعْ حَلَقةً بِإِذُنَك

Place it on your ear like an earring.

Follow what I say.

NOSE

مِنْخار : أنْفٌ

طالِعْ الأكِلِ مِن مَناخيري : الطَعامُ خارِجٌ مِنْ أنْفي

The food is coming out of my nose.

I am stuffed.

وُصْلِت معي لَراس مَناخيري : وَصَلَتْ معي لِرأسِ أنْفي

It has reached the top of my nose.

The problems are out of control and burdensome.

مَنَاخيرو عاليِه : أنْفُهُ مرتَفِعةٌ

His nose is high.

He is a snob.

FINGERS

أصابيع : أصابع

مو كِل أصابيعك مِتل بعِضْ : ليْسَ كلُّ الأصابعُ مثلَ بعضِها

Not all your fingers are the same.

Not every member of a family or society is the same; even if one person misbehaves, the rest of the group is not necessarily impolite.

مِثْلَ خاتِمٍ بأصبعا : مِثْلَ خاتِمٍ بِأصبعها

He is like a ring on her finger.

He is under her control.

إنتَ بِتِلعبْ بالنار وبوكرا راحْ تِحْرؤ أصابيعَك : أنتَ تَلْعَبُ بِالنارِ وَ غَداً سَتَحْرُقُ أصابِعَك

You are playing with fire and tomorrow you will burn your fingers.

You are taking unnecessary risks. Be careful!

رَح تاكُل أصابيعَك وَراها : سَتَأكُلُ أصابِعَكَ مِنْ بَعْدِها

It will make you eat your fingers.

The food is so delicious! You will love it!

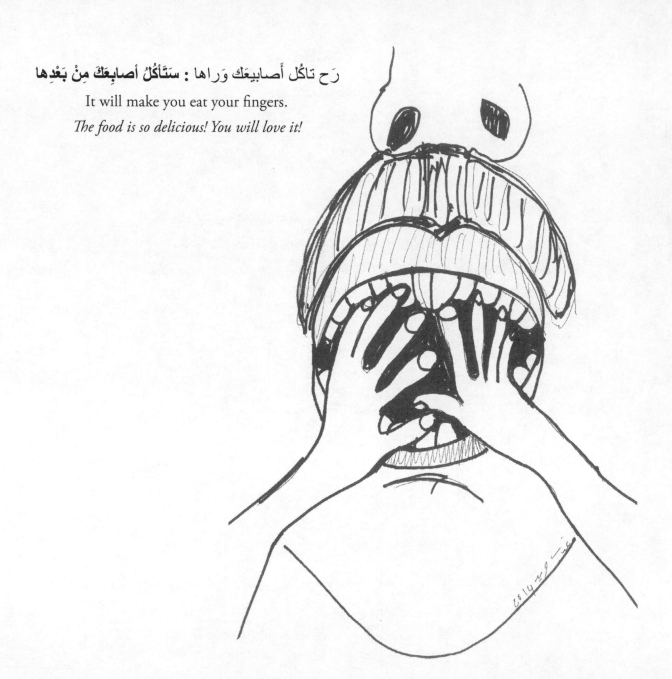

SKIN

البَشَرة

نامْ بكّير وفيئ بكّير وشوفْ بشرتَكْ (صحتَكْ) كيف بتصير :

نامْ باكِراً واسْتَيْقِظْ باكِراً وسَتَرى بُشْرَتَك (صحتَك) ... كَيْفَ تُصْبِحُ

Rise and shine early and see how lovely your complexion becomes!

Early to bed and early to rise makes a man healthy, wealthy, and wise.

STOMACH

البَطِن

عايشين بِنَفَس البَطِن وشُربانين نفسْ الحَلِيب : هُم عاشُوا في ذاتِ البَطِنِ وَشَرِبوا ذاتِ الحَلِيبَ

They lived in the same stomach and drank the same milk.

They were raised together, but look how different they are! Or depending on the context: Yes, of course they agree. They grew up together.

أله يِحْيي البَطِن لَّي حِملك : أللهُ يُحْيي البَطِنَ الذي حَمَلَكَ

God bless the stomach that carried you!

You are amazing! May God bless the woman who gave birth to you!

بَطْنُه كبير= كرُشه كبير : بَطْنُهُ كَبيرٌ

He has a big stomach.

Used to indicate a doctor, lawyer, or other well-paid professional, who charges too much and cheats clients.

البَطِن بسْتان : البَطنُ كَالبُسْتانِ

The womb is a garden filled with many kinds of flowers.

Just because siblings share the same mother does not mean they have anything in common.

مفتاح البَطِنِ لِنْمِه ومِفْتاح الشرْ كِلِمِه : مُفتاحُ البَطِنِ لُقْمَةٌ وَمُفتاحُ الشَرِ كَلِمَةٌ

The key to the stomach is one bite, and the key to evil is one word.

In the same way that one bite unlocks the appetite, one word can lead to evil.

22

عَصافير بَطْني عَمتزأزئ : عَصافيرُ بَطْني تُزَقْزِقُ

The birds in my stomach are chirping.

My stomach is grumbling. I am starving.

23

FOREHEAD

الجَبين

مِن عَرَأ جبَيني : مِن عَرَقِ جَبيني

From the sweat of my forehead.

I accomplished this through my own effort.

لَّي نْكَتَب عالجُبين لازِم تْشوفو العَيْن : المَكتوبُ على الجَبينِ يَجِبُ أن تَراهُ العَيْن (القَدَر)

That which is written on the cheek, the eye must see.

Destiny influences people's lives.

THE BODY

البَدَن : الجَسَد

خَبَر بيسمُّ البَدَنْ = شي بيهِزْ البَدَن : خَبَرٌ يهُزُّ الجسَدَ

News that poisons the body

What horrible news!

عاده بالبَدَن ما بيغَيِّرا غَيْر الكَفَن : عادَةٌ بالجَسَدِ لا تتَغَيَّرْ إلاّ بِالكَفَنِ (المَوْت)

Habits in the body don't change until the grave.

Habits only die when we die.

BLOOD

الدَمْ

دمُه تنَيل : **دمُهُ ثَقيلٌ**

He has thick blood.

He is a bore.

دمُه خَفيف : **دَمُهُ خَفيفٌ**

He has light blood.

He has a great sense of humor.

أنا من لَحْم ودَم : **أنا مُكَوَّنٌ مِن لَحمٍ وَدَمٍ**

I am made of meat and blood.

I am human.

الدَم ما بيصير ماي : **الدَمُ لا يَتَحَوَّلُ إلى ماءٍ**

Blood does not become water.

Used in a context when relatives may be fighting and someone wants to make peace; they say that they have blood in common, meaning they must unite.

BRAIN

دِماغْ = مُخْ

هوِّ ذَكي بَس مُخُه مو مَعُه : هوَ ذَكيٌّ لَكنَ دِماغَهُ ليسَ مَعَهُ

He is smart but his brain is not with him.

He is smart but has no common sense.

ما في مُخْ : لا يوجدُ مُخٌّ

There is no brain.

Describes someone who is not acting wisely

مُخُّه مسَكَّرْ : مُخُهُ مُغْلَقٌ

His head is closed.

He is closed-minded.

BEARD

دأنُه : ذَقنُه

واحَدْ حامِلْ دأنُه والتاني تعْبان فيها : واحَدّ حامِلٌ ذَقنَهُ والآخرُ تَعبانٌ فيها

One man is sporting a beard and others are tiring themselves over it.

People keep interfering with one individual's concerns.

HEAD

راس : رأس

حامِل السلّم بالعَرِض وما بيعمِل إلا ّ لّي براسُه : **هو حامِلٌ السلّمَ بالعَرضِ ولا يَعْمَلُ إلا ما يُفَكِّرُ بِهِ**

He is carrying the ladder by the side and he will only do what is in his head.

He will do exactly what he wants no matter what you say.

ما في حداً يْئب راسه : لا يَسْتَطيعُ أَحَدٌ أَن يَرْفَعَ رَأْسَهُ

No one is raising his head.

No one can hold his head up with pride here.

ما بيساوي إلاّ لّي بِراسُه : لا يَعْمَلُ إلاّ الذي يُفَكّرُ فيه

He will only do what is in his head.

He will do exactly as he pleases.

الشيطان بيلعَبْ بالراس : الشَيْطانُ يَلْعَبُ في الرَأسِ

The devil plays with the mind.

Used in a context when someone has behaved badly and when he apologizes, he says the devil played with his head.

حُطُّ راسَك بيْن الروس و وُّول يا أَطْاع الروس : ضَعْ رأسَكَ بيْنَ الروَّوسِ وقُلْ يا قُطّاعَ الروَّوسِ

Put your head among the other heads and call out, "cut off our heads."

Do as others do. All will face the same consequences. (This is used in a metaphorical sense in a society with a political dictatorship. It attests to a widespread feeling of resignation.)

الفَئير لّي راسُه مَرْفوع أفضَل من الغَني لّي بإيدُه كَلَبْشات :
الفَقيرُ الذي رأسُهُ مَرْفوعٌ خَيرٌ مِن الغَنِّي الذي بِيَدِهِ كَلَبْشاتٍ

A poor individual with a head held high is better than a rich person with chains on his hands.

Better to be honest and poor than risk stealing and imprisonment.

سُبحان لَي بيوَفِّئ راسَيْن على فرْدْ مخدّة : سُبْحانَ مَن يُوَفِّقُ رأسَيْن عَلى نَفسِ الوِسادةِ

Wow! See how they put their heads on the same pillow.

Look how harmonious this couple is.

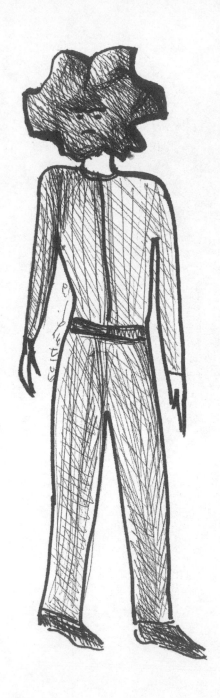

راسُه متل الحَجَر : رَأسُهُ مثلَ الحَجَرِ

His head is like a rock.

He is very stubborn.

شايِل كِل الشُغِل فَوْء راسُه : **حامِلٌ كلُ الشُغلِ فَوْقَ رأسِهِ**

He is carrying all the work over his head.

He is bearing all the responsibility for the work.

الشُغل مكوَّم فَوْء راسي = الشُغل فَوْء راسي : **الشُغْلُ فَوْقَ رأسي**

Work is gathering above my head.

I have an unspeakable amount of work to get done.

ما حداً عَراسُه خِيمِه : **لا أَحَدُ عَلى رأسِهِ خَيْمَة**

No one has a tent on his head.

No one is safe.

خايِف كإنُه عَراسُه طَيْر : **خائفٌ كَأنَّ عَلى رَأسِهِ طائر**

He is scared as if there is a bird on his head.

He is very still, afraid to move.

بْحُطْها عَراسي من فَوْء : **أضَعُها عَلى رَأسي مِن فَوْقٍ**

I will put her on top of my head.

Don't worry. I will take very good care of her.

عَراسي : **عَلى رَأسي**

On my head.

My pleasure; I would be happy to fulfill your request.

شي بيِرفَع الراس : شَيْءٌ يَرفَعُ الرَأسَ

Something that lifts up the head.

A cause for pride

شي بيوَطّي الراس : شَيْءٌ يُحني الرَأسَ

Something that lowers the head.

Something shameful

حَأَك عَراسي من فَوْء : حَقُّكَ عَلى رَأسي مِن فَوْقٍ

That which you deserve is on the top of my head.

I owe you and of course will do as you ask.

وَجِعِتْ راس : شَيْءٌ يُوَجِّعُ الرأسَ

Something that will hurt the head.

Something that will cause a headache.

ما بيَعرِف راسُه مِنْ رجليْه : لا يَعْرِفُ رَأسَهُ مِن رِجْلَيْه

He does not know his legs from his head.

He is so confused!

لّي بيُطْلَعْ لَفَوْء بينكسِر راسُه : مَن يَطلَعُ لِفَوْقٍ يَنْكَسِرُ رأسَهُ

He who climbs high will have his head broken.

Don't be too ambitious or the political powers will feel threatened and rip you up.

أنتَ تاج راسي : **أنتَ سيّدُ رأسي**

You are the crown of my head.

You are everything to me.

أله يْديمَكْ فَوْء راسي : أللهُ يُديمْكَ فَوْقَ رأسي

May God keep you over my head.

May God protect you.

لّي إلو عْيون وراسْ بيَعمِل مِتل ما بيَعملو الناس : الذي لَهُ عُيونٌ وَرأسٌ يَعْملُ كما يَعْملُ الناسُ

Someone who has eyes and a head will do as other people do.

It is best to conform in order to stay out of trouble.

عَألُه براسُه و بيَعرِف خلاصُه : عَقْلُهُ في رَأسِهِ وَيَعرِفُ خَلاصَهُ

His brain is in his head and he knows his interests.

He has a good head on his shoulders.

خَلّي راسَكْ بارِد : إبقي رَاسَكَ بارِداً

Keep your head cold.

Stay calm.

بْحُطّ شي بِراسي : أضَعُ شَيءاً في رَاسي

I put something in my head.

Once I have a goal, I see it through.

حْتُرْنا يا أءرَعْ مِن وَيْن نْمَشْطَكْ : إحْتَرْنا يا أقْرَعْ مِن أيْنَ نُمَشّطُكَ

Oh, bald man! We are so confused. Where should we brush?

We don't really know how to deal with you.

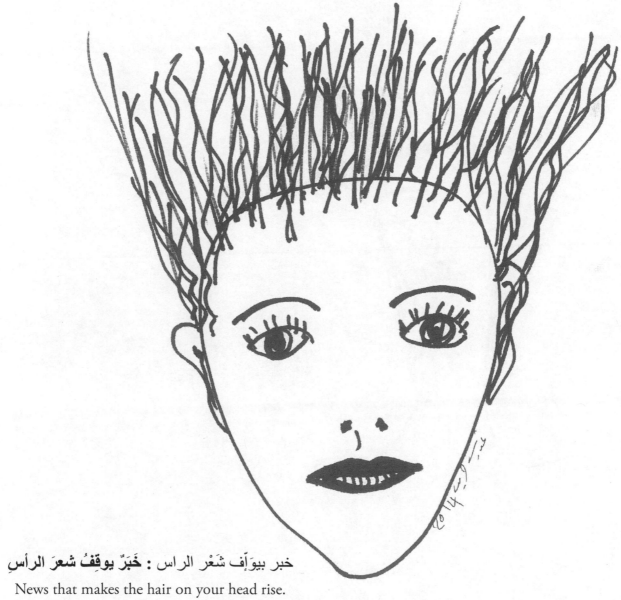

خبر بيوَاّف شَعْر الراس : خَبَرٌ يوقِفُ شعرَ الرأسِ

News that makes the hair on your head rise.

Shocking news

على رأسِها ريشةٌ : على راسا ريشه

On her head is a peacock feather.

She is a real snob.

38

LEGS

إجِر : رِجْلٌ

أنا الرِجَال أو إجِر كُرسي؟ : أَأَنا رَجُلٌ أَمْ رِجْلَ كُرسيٍّ؟

As soon as the cow falls and breaks his legs everyone will attack him.

Do I have any say as the man of the house?

بسْ البَأرَه بتوأع وبتنكِسِر إِجرا الكِل عَلِيا بْيهْجُمْ : عِنْدَما تَقَعُ البَقَرَةُ وَتَكْسِرُ رِجلَها الكُلُ يَهْجُمُ عَلَيْها

As soon as the cow falls and breaks his legs everyone will attack him.

As soon as a person demonstrates weakness, everyone will take advantage.

بس البَأرَه بتوأع بِيكْتَرُه سُلّاخينا : عِنْدَما تَقَعُ البَقَرَةُ يَكثُرُ مَن سَيَسْلُخُها

As soon as the cow falls, those who want to skin it increase in number.

As soon as someone is in a weak position, everyone will take advantage.

وَأَفْ عَرِجْلَيْه : وقَفَ على رجلَيْهِ

He is standing on his own legs.

He is capable and independent.

ماشْيِي الماي من تحِت إجرَيْه : الماءُ تَمُرُّ مَنْ تَحْت رِجْلَيْهِ

Water is running under his legs.

Things are going on behind his back.

إجِر بِماي و إجِر بِنار : رِجلٌ بِالماءِ وَرِجِلٌ بِالنارِ

He has one leg in water and another in fire.

He does not know what to do.

إِجِر بِالفلاحة وإِجِر بِالبور : رِجْلٌ في الفلاَحَةِ وَرِجْلٌ في البورِ

One leg is on the ground the farmer has cultivated for harvest; the other is on uncultivated land.

Describes someone who is hesitant.

مِدّ بساطَك أد إِجرَيْك : أفْرُشْ سجادَتَكَ عَلى قَدَرِ رِجْلَيْكَ

Lay out the carpet as long as your leg can reach.

Be realistic about what you want.

NECK

رَأَبِة : رَقَبَةٌ = عُنق

مِن عْضام الرَأَبِة : مِن عِظامِ الرَقْبَةِ

From the bones in the neck

Describes someone linked to the regime

أمانِه بِرَأَبتي : أمانَةٌ في رَقْبَتي

A trust that is placed in my neck

I will take care of that which has been entrusted to me.

دَيْن بِرَأَبتي : دَيْنٌ في رقبتي

A debt on my neck

A debt I must repay

حُطْها بِرأَبتي : ضَعْها في رَقْبَتي

I will put her on my neck.

I will take care of her.

بيْمون عَرأَبتي : يَمونُ عَلى رَقْبَتي

He can place an order on my neck.

His wish is my command.

SOUL

الروح

طْلَعتِلّي روحي : طَلَّعْتَ لي روحي

He pulled out my soul.

He irritated the hell out of me.

حاسِس روحي عمتُطْلَع : أَشْعُرُ بِأَنَّ روحي تطلُعُ

I feel as if my soul is going to come out.

I've had it!

صَديء مِنْ الروح للروح : صَديقٌ مِنَ الروحِ لِلْروحِ

A friend, soul to soul.

A friend who is a soul-mate.

MUSTACHE

الشارِبُ

بِشْواربي : بِشَوارِبي

On my mustache

On my honor

حَياة شْواربي : وَحَياةُ شَوارِبي

For the life of my mustache

I swear on my honor.

ألله يحيي شْواربَك : اللهُ يُحيي شَوارِبَك

May God make your mustache live!

Long live your honor and manliness.

تُكرَم شْواربَك : تُكرم شَوارِبَك

May your mustache be blessed.

Yes, I will do this, on your honor.

HAIR

الشعرُ

بيُطْلع مِتل الشعرَه من العَجين : يَخْرُجُ مثلَ الشَعرةِ مِنَ العَجينِ

He gets out like hair from dough.

He gets out of the problem unscathed.

FINGERNAILS

ضُفِر (ضَفير) : ظُفِر (أظافِر)

ما بيحِك جِلْدَك غير ضُفرَك : لا يحُكُّ جِلْدَك غيْر أظافِرِك

Only your own fingernails can scratch your skin.

Only you know what is best for yourself.

46

BACK

الضَهِرْ : الظَهْرُ

إرمي ورا ضَهْرَك : إرْمي خَلْفَ ظَهْرِكَ

Throw it behind your back.

Forget about it.

هَيْدا كسَّرلي ضَهْري : هذا كسَّرَ لي ظهري

That broke my back.

That really exhausted and pained me.

ما في وَراةْ ضَهِر : لَيْسَ خَلْفَهُ ظَهْراً (سَنَداً)

There is no back behind him.

There is no one in power protecting him.

وراةْ ضَهِر : وراءَهُ ظهرٌ

There is a back behind him.

Someone in power is protecting him.

خَلّيه يْحِسّ وراةْ ضِهِر : دَعْهُ يَشْعُرُ أنَّ خَلْفَهُ ظَهِرٌ

Let him feel as if there is a back behind him.

Let him feel as if someone is protecting him.

BONES

العَضِم : العَظْمُ

أكَلُه لحِم و رَماه عَضِم : أكَلَهُ لَحِماً وَرماهُ عَظماً

He ate his meat and threw away the bones.

He really took advantage of that person.

اللحِم إلِك و العَضم إلي : اللَحْمُ لَكَ وَالعَظْمُ لي

The meat is for you and the bones are for me.

You get the best part.

أنا مِش الطَيْر لّي بيتِّاكَل لَحْمُه و بينْتِركْ عْضامُه : أنا لَسْتُ الطَيْرَ الذي يوكَلُ لَحْمَهُ وتُتْرَكُ عظامَهُ

I am not a bird whose meat is eaten and whose bones are left over.

I am not someone you can take advantage of.

بَيْت السَبِع ما بيخْلى مِن لِعْضام : بَيْتُ السَبْعِ لا يَخلو مِنَ العِظامِ

The lion's den is never missing any bones.

This is a home that always has food because the inhabitants work hard for it.

BRAIN

العَإلْ : العَقْلُ

عَاله بيوزِن بَلَدْ : عَقْلُهُ يُوزِنُ بَلَداً

His brain is as big as the country.

He is very smart.

بدّي أشاوِر عَالي : أريدُ أنْ أُشاوِرَ عَقْلي

I need to discuss with my mind.

I need to think about this.

العَئِل زينِةْ بَني آدم : العَقْلُ زينَةُ الإنْسانِ

The mind is the greatest décor of the human being.

Wisdom is the most important attribute of the human being.

العَئِل لِكبير بيِسْتَوْعِب العَئِل لِصغير : العَقْلُ الكَبيرُ يَسْتَوْعِبُ العَقْلَ الصَغيرَ

A large mind can deal with the smaller mind.

A wise person is able to figure out how to deal with the silly ones.

العَئِل السَليم بالجِسم السَليم : العَقْلُ السَليمُ في الجِسمِ السَليمِ

A healthy mind in a healthy body.

إللي بيجَرِّب المُجَرَّب بيكوْن عَأله مُخَرَّب : الذي يُجَرِّبُ المُجَرَّبُ يَكونُ عَقْلُهُ مُخَرَّباً

He who experiences that which he has already experienced has a wrecked mind.

He who relives the same bad experience is stupid.

الجاهِل بيتْعَلَّم من كيسُه والعائل مِن كيس غَيْرُه : الجاهِلُ يَتَعَلَّمُ مِن كيسِهِ والعاقِلُ مِن كيسِ غَيْرِهِ

The ignorant one learns from his own bag while the wise one learns from the bags of others.

The ignorant one learns from his own experiences while the wise one learns from others' experiences.

عَئِل عُطيني وبالبَحر رْميني : عَقْلٌ أعْطيني وَبِالبَحرِ إرْميني

Give me a mind and throw me into the sea.

Make me wise and I can handle anything.

شي بياخُد العئِل = بيطيِّر العئل : شَيءٌ يأخُذُ العَقلَ = شيْءٌ يُطَيِّرُ العَقلَ

Something that blows away the mind

Describes something astonishing.

عَيْن العئِل = زينة العئِل : عَيْنُ العَقلِ

The eye of the mind

Such incredible wisdom

عَأله خَفيف = إلّة العئِل = عَأله صغير : عَقْلُهُ صغيرٌ

He has a light mind.

He is not a wise person.

عَألَه كبير : عَقْلُهُ كَبيرٌ

His mind is huge.

He is exceptionally wise.

عَألَه بيوَزّع عَبَلَدْ : عَقْلُهُ يُوَزِّع على بَلَد

His mind spreads far.

He is exceptionally wise.

كَبِّر عَألَك = خَلّي عَألَك بِراسَك = خَلّي عَألَك كبير : دَعْ عَقلَك في رأسِكَ

Make your mind large; put your mind in your head.

Be wise.

رِجِع لعَألَه : رَجِعَ لِعَقْلِهِ

He came back to his mind.

He came back to his senses.

عَألَه بِبَطْنَه : عَقْلُهُ بِبَطْنِهِ

His mind is in his stomach.

He thinks only of food.

عِمِل عَيْن العئل : عَمِلَ عَيْنَ العَقْلِ

He did the eye of the mind.

He did the wisest thing.

51

شَغْلِه بِتْخلّي العَئِل بالكَفْ : شَيءٌ يَدَعُ العَقْلَ بالكَفِ

Something that puts the mind in the palms of the hand.

Something very confusing.

كل واحَد حُرّ بِعَأله : كُلُّ واحِدٍ حرٌّ بِعَقْلِهِ

Everyone is free in their mind.

Everyone can do what they feel is wise.

راح آخْدَك عَأدْ عَألَك : سآخذُكَ على قدرِ عقلِكَ

I will deal with you at the level of your mind.

I will deal with you at your own level.

عنْدْ البُطونْ ضاعِتْ العُؤول : عِنْدَ البُطونِ ضاعَتِ العُقولَ

With the stomach, the minds were lost.

Once everyone sat down to eat, they stopped thinking.

NECK

العِنئ : العُنُقُ

أطْعْ الأرزاء مِن أطْع الأعْناء : قَطْعُ الأرْزاقِ مِن قَطْعِ الأعْناقِ

If you cut their livelihood you cut their neck.

Cutting off someone's livelihood is like killing him.

EYES

العَيْن

بِفرِشْلَك ريف عيوني : أَفْرُشُ لَكَ ريفَ عُيوني

I will lay out my eyelashes for you.

There is no limit to what I will give you.

لَّي بيشوفَك بِعَيْن بِتشوفُه بِتنَيْن : الذي يَراكَ بِعَيْنٍ تَراهُ بِإثْنَيْن

He who sees you with one eye, you see with two eyes.

If someone has given you something, you'll give back two-fold.

عَيْن لَّي بِتحِب عَميا : العَيْنُ التي تُحِبُ عَمْياءٌ

The eye of he who loves is blind.

Love is blind.

العَيْن بالعَيْن والسِن بالسِنْ : العَيْنُ بالعَيْنِ والسِنُّ بالسِّنِّ

An eye for an eye and tooth for a tooth

What goes around comes around.

الإرِد بِعَيْن إمّه غَزال : القِردُ بِعَيْنِ أمّه غَزالٌ

A monkey is a gazelle in his mother's eyes.

Beauty is in the eye of the beholder.

إذا فِتِتْ عَبَلَدْ عُوران حُطْ إيدَك عَيْنَك : إذا دَخَلْتَ إلى بَلدٍ عورانٍ ضَعْ يَدَكَ على عَيْنِكَ

If you enter a country where people have only one eye, cover one of your eyes.

When in Rome, do as the Romans do.

بايِنْ مِتِل عَيْن الشَمِسْ : واضِحٌ مِثْلَ عَيْنِ الشَمِسِ

It is clear as the eye of the sun.

It is evident.

شِبْعان لَعَيْنُه : عيونُهُ شِبْعانةٌ

His eyes are full.

He is a completely satisfied person.

يْعَبّي العَيْن : يَمْلأُ العَيْنَ

He fills the eyes.

He is so well-loved.

دَخيلْ عَيْنَك = تسْلَمْلي عَيْنَك : تَسْلَمُ لي عيْنُكَ

Bless you! Or, Please!

بحُطّها بِعيوني = بخَلّيها بِعْيوني = بحْمِلْها بِعيوني : أضَعُها في عُيوني

I will put her in my eyes.

I will take very good care of her.

55

لَعيوني = عَيْني = عَيْني وْراسي = من عيوني لِتْنَيْن = تِكْرَمْ عيونَكْ :
على عَيْني وَرَأسي = مِن عُيوني الإِثْنَيْن

For my eyes; on my eyes; on my eyes and head; on my two eyes; bless your eyes

Yes of course, I would be happy to help you.

ألله يْعينَكْ : **ألله يُعينُك**

May God give you eyes.

May God give you strength in such tough circumstances.

أنا شبْعان وما بْعَيْني شي : **أنا شَبْعانٌ وَلَيْسَ بعَيْني شَيْء**

I am full and there is nothing in my eyes.

I am completely satisfied.

هوِّ شِبْعان وما في بِعيونه شي : **هُوَ شَبْعانٌ وَلَيْسَ في عَيْنَيْه شَيْء**

He is full and there is nothing in his eyes.

He is completely satisfied.

عيونُه ما بيِشْبِعا غَيْر الدودْ : **عيونَهُ لا يُشْبِعْها إلا الدودْ (عُيونَهُ لا تَشْبَعْ إلا عِنْدَ المَوْت)**

His eyes will only be satisfied when faced with worms.

Refers to a covetous individual who will only be satisfied once faced with death.

بِيْعِيْنْ الله : أَللهُ يُعينُ

In the eyes of God

God knows best why I am going through hardship.

طَيَّرْ النَوْم مِن عيوني : طَيَّرَ النَوْمَ مِن عُيوني

Sleep flew from his/eyes. *my*

He is no longer tired.

وِحْياة عْيونَكْ : وَحَياةُ عُيونُكَ

For the life of your eyes

I swear.

عَيْني مِحْمَرَّة مِنَّكْ : عَيْني مِحْمَرَّةٌ مِنْكَ

My eyes are red because of you.

You've made me so mad.

شو بَدّو الأعمى ....جَوْز عيون : ماذا يُريدُ الأعمى سِوى زوجَ عيونٍ

What does the blind person want? Just a pair of eyes.

Something that you need very much.

عَيْن الله علَيْه : عَينُ أللهِ عَلَيْهِ

May God's eyes be upon you. *him*

May God protect you.

يا عَيْن عَلَيْكَ : يا عَيْن عَلَيْكَ

Oh, an eye on you!

Bravo!

العَيْن مفتَّحة عَلَيْنا : العَيْنُ مُفَتَّحةٌ عَلَيْنا

Eyes are open on us.

Everyone is watching us.

بِخزي العَيْن عَنَّكَ : يَمْنَعُ العينَ عنْكَ

Take the eye away from you.

Keep the evil eye away from you.

العَمى بِعيونَكَ : العَمى في عُيونِكَ

May your eyes be blinded.

Curse on you.

بَعيد عَن العَيْن بَعيد عَن الألب : بَعيدٌ عَنِ العَيْنِ بَعيدٌ عَنِ القَلبِ

Far from the eyes, far from the heart

When the beloved is far awa, he or she is forgotten.

بيْضَل بِعَيْني زْغير : يَبقى في عَيْني صَغيراً

He will always remain small in my eyes.

My child will always remain a child in my eyes.

58

بيِسْرُوْ الكُحل مِن العَيْن : يَسْرُقُ الكحْلَ مِنَ العَيْنِ

He steals the *kohl* from under the eyes.

He is a crafty thief.

إنتَ بِتْتَعِّب العَين : أنتَ تُتَعِّبُ العَيْنَ

You tire the eyes.

You are exhausting.

ما تْخاف على الطِفُل مِنْ عُيون إمِّه و أبوه : لا تَخافْ عَلى الطفْلِ مِن عُيونِ أمِّهِ وأبيهِ

Do not fear the impact of the eyes of the mother and father on the child.

Parents will not bring the evil eye to their own child.

أنتَ نورْ عْيوني : أنتَ نورَ عُيوني

You are the light of my eyes.

You are the light of my life.

العَيْن بَصيرة واليَدْ أصيرَة : العَيْنُ بَصيرَةٌ وَاليَدُ قَصيرَةٌ

The eye sees and the hand is small.

Describes a person who wants something unattainable

أغْلى مِن نورْ عْيوني : أغْلى مِن نورِ عُيوني

Dearer to me than the light of my eyes

Someone is more special to me than anything else

كذّاب بِنُصّ عَيْنُه : هُوَ كَذّابٌ في نِصْفِ عَيْنِهِ

He is a liar in the middle of his eye.

He is not afraid to lie to your face.

عَيْن ما بِتأشَعْ ألبْ ما بْيوجَعْ : عَيْنٌ لا تَقشَعْ (تَرى) قَلْبٌ لا يوجَعْ (يَتَأَلَّمْ)

That which the eye does not see does not cause the heart pain.

If something painful is far from your eyes, then you will not suffer.

THE MIND

البال: الفِكِر

الصبِر وطولِة البال عند بَني آدم بيوازي جَبَلْ : **الصَبرُ وَطولَةِ البالِ عِنْدَ الإنْسانِ تُساوي جَبَلاً**

Patience is like a mountain.

Patience makes a person as strong as a mountain.

إبْن الحَلال بينْذَكر بالبال \ بنْتْ الحَلال بتنْذَكر بالبال : **الرَجُلُ الجَيِّدُ أو الإمرَأةُ الجَيِّدَةُ نَتَذَكّرْهُمْ بالفِكِرِ**

A good person comes to mind.

You came right when we were talking so highly about you!

ألله يْرَيِّحْ بالَك = ما يِغْلي ألبَكْ = ما بِنْشَغِل بالَك : **يا ليتَ اللهَ يُرَيِّحُ فِكْرَكَ**

May God ease your mind.

شَغِلْتلّي بالي : **شَغَلْتَ لي فِكْري**

You worked my mind.

You worried me!

تُخْطُر بِبالَك : **تأتي على فكرِكَ**

It came to mind.

61

MOUTH

التِّمّ : الفَمُ

ترميه بالبَحر بيطْلعْ بيتمُّه سمْكة : تَرميهِ في البَحرِ يَخْرُجُ وَيوجَدُ في فَمِهِ سَمَكة

Throw him into the sea and he will come out with fish in his mouth.

Even when you put him in a hard situation, he comes out ahead.

62

في بتِمَّك حَكي : يوجَدُ في فَمِك كَلامٌ

There are words in your mouth.

It seems you have something you really want to say.

يِسْلَمْ هَالتَمّ لَّي بينإَّط عسل : يَسْلَمُ هذا الفَمُ الذي يُنقِّطُ عسَلاً

May God bless the mouth from which honey drips.

What a sweet thing to say!

يِسْلَمْ تِمَّك : يَسْلَمُ فَمَكَ

Bless your mouth

What a wonderful thing to say!

جَيْتَك أحلى مِن العَسَل عَالتَمّ : مَجيئَكَ أفضَلُ مِنَ العَسَلِ عَلى الفَم

Your presence is more beautiful than honey in the mouth.

Seeing you here is more wonderful than anything else.

مِنْ تمَّك لَباب السما : مِنْ فَمِكَ لِباب السَماءِ

From your mouth to the door of the sky.

May God hear what you just said and make it come true.

صُرْنا متل العِلْكة في تِمّ الناس : أَصْبَحْنا مَثلَ العِلْكةِ في فَم الناسِ

We have become like gum in everyone's mouth.

Everyone is gossiping about us.

إِطْعَم التِمِّ بتِسْنْتِحي العَيْن :
أطْعِمْ الفَمَ تَخْجَلُ العَيْنَ

Give food to the mouth and the eyes will be embarrassed.

This is an expression referring to bribery. The idea is that if you slip some money under the table the recipient would be embarrassed not to fulfill your request.

ما حَداً باس تِمّا غيْر إمّا : لَمْ يُقبّلْ فمَها سِوى أمِها

No one has kissed her lips but her mom.

She is so innocent!

وِصْلِت اللئمِة للتِمّ : وصَلَتْ اللقْمَةُ للفَم

The food has almost reached my mouth.

I have almost reached my goal.

لا مِنْ تِمُّه وَلا مِنْ كِمُّه : لَيْسَ مِنْ فَمِهِ وَلا مِن كُمِّهِ

Not from his mouth and not from his sleeve.

He said nothing. He did nothing. He has nothing to do with what happened.

خِلّانَ و بْتِمُّه مَعْلأة مِنْ دَهَبْ : وُلِدَ وَفي فَمِه مِلعَقةً منْ ذهبٍ

He was born with a golden spoon in his mouth.

He grew up wealthy.

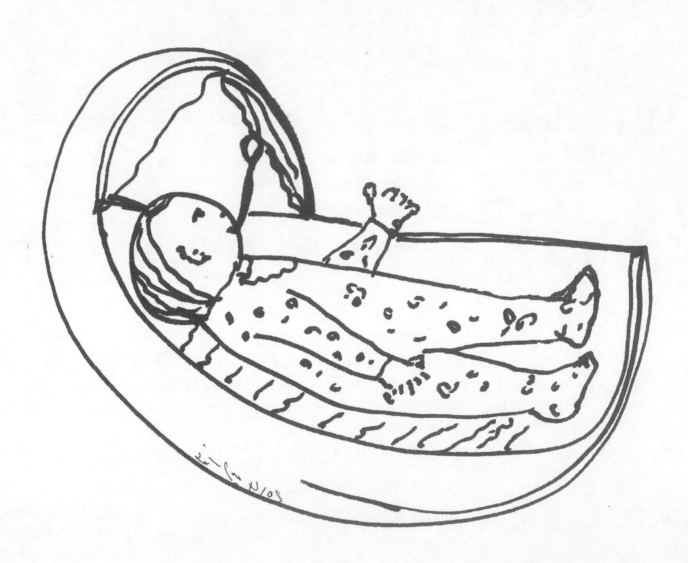

THE HEART

الأَلْبُ : القَلْبُ

لَي ما عِنْدُه مَصاري بينام من ألْبُه : الذي لَيْسَ لَدَيْهِ فُلوساً يَنامُ من قَلْبِهِ

One who has no money sleeps with all his heart.

One without money is free from all the problems of life.

صَفّي ألبَكْ ونيْتَكْ : صَفّي قَلْبَكَ وَنيَّتَكَ

Clear your mind and intentions.

Keep your intentions pure.

لَّي بِألبي عَراس لْساني : الذي في قَلْبِي هوَ عَلى رأسِ لِساني

That which is in my heart is on the tip of my tongue.

I said exactly what was on my mind.

نْحَرَأ ألبي عْلَيْه : إنحرَقَ قلبي علَيْهِ

My heart burnt because of him.

I am so worried about him.

ألبي عَمْيِغْلي عَلَيْه مِتلْ النارْ = ألبي شِعْلانْ عَلَيْه : قَلبي يَغْلي عَلَيْهِ مِثلَ النارِ

My heart is boiling for him like fire.

I am so worried about him.

نَفَخْتِلِّي أَلبِي : نَفَخْتَ لِي قَلبِي

You blew up my heart (like a balloon).

You've really frustrated me.

نِزلِتْ عَألبِي مِتِلْ السُكَّر = دابْ بِألبِي متِلْ السُكَّرَه : نَزَلَتْ عَلى قَلبِي مِثلَ السُكَّرِ = ذابَ في قَلبِي مِثلَ السُكَّر

She descended upon my heart like sugar.

I felt such a wonderful rapport with this individual.

دَخَل عَألبِي متِلْ النَسمِه : دَخَلَ عَلى قَلبِي مِثلَ النَسَمةِ

He entered my heart like a wind.

I really like this person.

ما حداً بِيَعْرِف شو بالألب إلاّ صْحَابْها : لا أَحَدٌ يَعلمُ ما في القلبِ إلاّ أصحابِها

No one knows what is in the heart but the possessor of the heart.

No one knows what others are really thinking.

ألبُه أسوَدْ : قَلْبُهُ أسوَدٌ

His heart is black.

He keeps grudges.

ألبُه أبيَضْ = ألبُه أبيض متلْ التلجْ : قَلْبُهُ مِثلَ الثلجِ

His heart is white. His heart is like snow.

He's a forgiving person.

مُفْتاح أَلْب الرَجُل بَطْنُه : مفتاحُ قلبُ الرجلِ بَطْنُه

The key to a man's heart is his stomach.

The way to a man's heart is through his stomach.

أَلله يْطَمِّنْ أَلبَك : أَلله يُطَمْئِنُ قَلْبَك

May God ease your heart.

May God relax you

بْعيد الشرْ عَن أَلبَك : بَعيدٌ الشَرُ عَن قَلْبِك

May evil be far from your heart.

May God protect you.

أَلبي بيحِسْ فيك : قَلبي يُحِسُ فيك

My heart feels for you.

I understand what you are going though.

سَلامِةُ أَلبَك : سَلامَةُ قَلْبُك

God bless your heart.

Feel better.

شي بِأطِّع الألِب : شيءٌ يُقطِّعُ القلبَ

Something that cuts the heart

Refers to something that breaks the heart

بِألبُه هَمْ : في قَلبِهِ هَمٌّ

In his heart is a concern.

He is worried about something.

ألوبْنا مَع بَعِضْ : قُلوبُنا مَع بَعْضٍ

Our hearts are with each other.

We stand with each other.

تؤبُر ألبي : تَقبُرُ قَلبي

Bury my heart.

I love this person so much.

أبوسْ ألبَكْ (أبوسْ روحَكْ) : أُقبّلُ قَلبَكَ

I kiss your heart.

I beg you.

خَلّي ألبُه يْحِسْ : دَعْ قَلْبَهُ يَحُسُّ

Let your heart feel.

Show compassion.

صَحْتَيْن عَألبَك : صَحْتَيْن عَلى قَلْبِك

Two healths on your heart!

Bon appétit!

ألبَك بارِدْ : قَلْبُكَ بارِدٌ

Your heart is cold.

You are a cool and unaffected person

أَعَدْ عَأَلْبِي : قَعَدَ عَلى قَلبي

He is sitting on my heart.

He is really irritating me.

ما تبَرِّدْ ألبَك : لا تُبَرِّدْ قَلْبَك

Don't make your heart grow cold.

Don't lose your compassion.

هوِّ أَريب من الألب : هوَ قَريبٌ مِنَ القلبِ

He is close to the heart.

I feel so comfortable with him.

ألبي وُصِلْ لإَجْري : قَلْبي وَصَلَ لِرِجْلي

My heart has reached my legs.

I am scared.

خَلِّيها بالألب تِجرَح وَلا تِحْكيها وتِفْضَحْ : أُتْرُكْها في القَلْبِ تَجْرَحْ وَلا تحْكيها وَتَفْضَحُ

Better to keep your secret in your heart and feel pain than to talk about it and cause a scandal.

رَبَّك ربْ الألوب : رَبُّك يَعْلَمُ ما في داخِلِ القُلوبِ

Your God is the God of hearts.

God knows what is in the heart.

SHOULDER

كَتِفْ

بَلَّشو يْشيلو الكِتِفْ عَنّي : بَدَأوا يَرْفَعوا الكَتِفَ عَنّي

They have started to take the shoulder off of me.

They have started to lift some of my burdens.

خَيْرُه من كِتِف غَيْرُه : خَيْرُهُ مِن كَتِفِ غَيْرِهِ

His blessings are from the shoulders of others.

Others have really helped him get where he is today.

حامِلْ مَسؤوليات عَكتِفُه : حامِلٌ مَسؤولياتٌ عَلى كَتِفِهِ

He is carrying responsibilities on his shoulders.

He has a lot of responsibilities.

لَحِم كُتافي مِنْ خَيْرَكْ : لَحمُ أكتافي مِن خَيرِكَ

The meat on my back is from your blessings.

You gave me everything I have.

PALM

كَفّ

الدِني عَكَفْ عَفْريتْ : الدُنيا على كَفِّ عفْريتٍ

The world is in the palm of a little devil.

Life is crazy.

شي بيحُطّ العَئل بِكَفّ : شَيْءٌ يَضَعُ العَقلَ بِكَفٍّ

Something that puts the mind in the palms of the hands.

Something that is really confusing.

TONGUE

اللِسان

لِسانا طَويلٌ : لِسانُها طَويلٌ

She has a long tongue

Someone who curses and talks back (often used to describe a woman who talks back to her husband).

الله يُقطَعْ لِسانُه : أَللهُ يَقطَعُ لِسانَهُ

May God cut his tongue.

May God make him stop being so impolite.

نْرَبَطْ لِساني : إنْرَبَطَ لِساني

My tongue is tied.

I cannot say anything.

ضُبْ لِسانكْ بِحَلَأكْ = ضُبْ لِسانَكْ بِتمَّكْ : خَبِّىْ لِسانَكَ في فمِكَ (حَلقك)

Put your tongue in your mouth.

Be quiet.

جَوابُكَ عَراس لِسانَك : جَوابُكَ عَلى رأسِ لِسانِك

Your response is on the tip of your tongue.

You always answer back right away.

لسانُه بِننَّطُ عَسَل : لِسانُه يُنقِّطُ عَسَلاً

Honey drips from your tongue.

You talk in such a sweet way.

بَلى الإنْسان مِن اللسان : بَلاءُ الإنْسانِ مِنَ اللِسانِ

Human catastrophe comes from the tongue.

Catastrophe arises from gossip and idle talk.

أَلِف زلِّة أَدَم ولا زَلَّة لسانْ : أَلْفُ زلَّةُ قَدَمٍ وَلا زلَّةُ لِسانٍ

A thousand slips of the feet are better than one slip of the tongue.

Gossip leads to greater disaster than physically falling down.

FACE

الوِج (الوِش) : الوَجهُ

بابْ السَما سَكَّر بِوِجّي : بابُ السَماءِ سكَّرَ بِوَجهي

The door of heaven has closed in my face.

All doors have closed in my face.

وجَّكْ حِلو عليّي = وجَّكْ خَيْر عليّي : وجهُكَ خَيْرٌ علَيَّ

Your face brings me blessings.

You bring me luck.

شي بِبيّض الوِج : شَيْءٌ يُبَيِّضُ الوجه

Something that whitens the face

Describes something that makes you look good in front of others

شي بِسَوِّدْ الوِجْ : شَيْءٌ يُسَوِّدُ الوَجه

Something that makes the face black

Describes something that makes you look bad in front of others

وجَّكْ منوَّرْ = وجَّكْ مضَوّي : وَجهُكَ منَوَّرٌ

Your face is lighted.

You look happy.

آخِدْ وِجْ : آخِذٌ وجهاً

To take face

To feel very comfortable

يِسْلَملي هَالوِجْ : يَسْلَمُ لي هذا الوَجهُ

Bless your face.

Bless you.

وِجَّكْ أو ضَوْ الأَمَرْ؟ : وَجْهُكَ أمْ ضَوْءُ القمَرِ؟

Your face or the light of the moon?

I am not sure which is more beautiful: your face or the light of the moon?

بوِجْ الحَزينه تسَكَّرِت المْدينه : بوَجهِ الحَزينَةِ تسكَّرَتْ المَدينةُ

Sad faces closed the city.

Wherever he goes, all the doors are closed to him.

وجْ بيُوُطَعْ الرِزِء : وَجِةٌ يَقْطَعُ الرِزْق

A face that cuts off blessings

Someone who brings bad luck to one's prosperity

خلّي بيْتَك نضيف ما بْتَعرِفْ مين بيدوسو وخَلّي وجَكْ نضيفْ ما بْتَعرِف مين بيبوسو :
حافِظْ على نَظافَةٍ بيْتِكَ لأنَّكَ لا تَعْرِفُ مَن سَيَدوسَهُ وَحافِظْ عَلى نَظافَةٍ وَجهكَ لأنَّكَ لا تعرِفُ مَن سَيَبوسَهُ

Keep your house clean: you don't know who will visit. Keep your face clean: you do not know who will kiss it.

Always keep your surroundings and body clean. Be ready.

Hand

إيد : يَدٌّ

مَسَكُه بالإيدْ اللي بِتْوَجْعُه : مَسَكَهُ باليَدِ التي تؤلِمُهُ

He is holding him on the hand that hurts him.

He has found this man's weak point and is taking advantage of it.

لّي عايِز النار بيمْسِكا بإيداي : الذي يَحْتاجُ النارَ يُمْسِكُها بِيَدَيْهِ

He who wants fire can hold it with his hand.

He is willing to do anything to attain his goal.

إيدُه واصْلِه (إيدُه طايْلِه) : يَدُهُ تَصِلُ

His hand reaches out.

He has connections; he has a lot of money.

بيُزرمُطْ مِنْ بَيْن إيدَيّي مِتِلْ الرَمِلْ الناعِمْ : يَنْزَلِقُ مِنْ بَيْنِ يَدَيَّ مِثْلَ الرَمْلِ الناعِمِ

It slips out of my hands like soft sand.

I am not in control.

بيِنْزَلْ من إيدَيّي متل المايْ : يَنْزِلُ من يَدَيَّ مثْلَ الماءِ

It slips out of my hands like water.

I am not in control.

إيدي نْرَبَطِتْ : إنْرَبَطَتْ يدي

My hands are tied.

إيدْ وِحْدِه ما بِتْزَرِّفْ : يدٌ وحدُها لا تصَفِّقُ

You cannot clap with one hand.

You need a helping hand to do what you want (Two heads are better than one).

الحَياة متلْ عُصفور بإيدَكْ إذا شَدَّيْت علَيْه كْتير بتاتْلُه وإذا رَخَّيْتْ بيطير :
الحياةُ مثلَ عصفورٍ بيَدِكَ إذا ضغطْتَ عليه كَثيراً تقْتُلُهُ وإذا رخَّيْتَ يَطيرُ

Life is like a bird in your hand. If you hold it too tightly you will kill it and if you let go, it will fly away.

Life requires a delicate balance between risk-taking and caution.

المِفْتاحْ بإيدُه : المُفتاحُ بيَدِهِ

The key is in his hand.

It is completely in his control to change things.

إيدُه طَويلِه : يدُهُ طَويلةٌ

His hand is long.

He steals.

أبوسْ إيدَكْ : أُقبِّلُ يدُكَ

I kiss your hand.

I beseech you.

أنْتَ بَيْن أَيْدي أمينِه : أنت بيْنَ أيْدٍ أمينةٍ

You are in safe hands.

You are safe.

ما تمِدْ إيدَكْ عَلَيا : لا تَمدّ يدَكَ عليْها

Do not put your hand on her.

Do not hit her.

إنْشاالله ما بيِفْلَت من إيدي مَرَّة تانِيه : أن شاءَ اللهُ لا يَفْلتُ مِن يدي مرَّةً ثانيةً

God willing he/she will not escape my hands another time.

I hope I do not lose him/her again.

هُوِّ إيدي اليَمين : هُوَ يَدي اليَمين

He is my right hand man.

I depend on him for everything.

عَصْفورٌ بِالإيدْ وَلا عَشْرَة عَالشَجَرَه : عصفورٌ باليدِ ولا عَشْرةٌ على الشجرةِ

One bird in the hand is better than ten on a tree.

A bird in the hand is worth two in the bush.

إيدُه ماسْكَه : يدُهُ ماسِكَةٌ

His hand is tight.

He is stingy.

لَّي إيدُه بالماي مو مِتلْ لَّي إيدُه بالنار : الذي يدُهُ في الماءِ لَيْسَ مثْلَ مَن يدَهُ في النارِ

He whose hand is in water is not like he whose hand is in fire.

Someone in the midst of a crisis cannot be compared to someone in a relaxing situation.

لَّي بِيتِفَرَّجْ عَجَمْرَه حمْرا مو متلْ لَّي ماسِكا بإيدُه لَيْلْ نهارْ :
مَن يتفرَّجُ على جمْرةٍ حمْراءٍ ليْسَ مثلَ الذي يمْسِكُها بِيَدِهِ لَيْلاً ونَهاراً

He who is looking at a hot red coal can't be compared to he who is holding it night and day.

You cannot compare the person with problems with the person without problems.

حُطْ إيدَيْكْ و إجرَيْكْ بِماي بارِده : ضعْ يَدَيْكَ وَرِجْليْكَ في ماءٍ باردةٍ

Put your hands and legs in cold water.

Don't be stressed, stay calm about this.

لَي مِنْ إيدُه ألله يْزيدُه : الذي مِن يَدِهِ أللهُ يَزيدُهُ

May God increase that which he has done with his own hands.

God will help those who help themselves. (It can also be meant in the negative sense: God will increase the problems of him who brings problems on himself).

إذا كِتْرِت الأيادي بيحْترِء الأكِلْ : إذا كثُرَتْ الأيادي تَحْتَرِقُ الطبْخةَ

If there are too many hands then the food will burn.

Too many cooks spoil the broth.

أنا مِتل الخاتِمْ بَين إيدَيْكْ : أنا كالخاتِمِ بينَ يَدَيْكَ

I am like a ring in your hands.

I am completely under your control.

خَلّينا إيدْ وِحْدِه : فلْنَبْقى يَداً واحِدةً

Let's stay one hand.

Let's stay united.

شو طالِعْ بإيدي؟ : ماذا أستطيعُ أنْ أفعلَ

What is arising from my hands?

What can I do?

إِيدُه تَايِلِه : يدُهُ ثقيلةٌ

His hand is heavy.

Describes someone who gives shots that really hurt

خَلَّيْتَني لِعْبِه بَيْن إِيدَيْك = مِتلْ العَجين بين إِيدَكْ : جعَلْتَني لُعْبةً بين يَدَيْكَ = أنا مِثلَ العَجينِ بينَ يديْكَ

I am like dough in your hands/I am like a game in your hands.

I am completely under your control.

ضيَّعْت جَوْهَرَه من بَيْن إِيدَيْك : أضعْتَ جوْهَرَةً مِنْ بينَ يديْكَ

You lost a jewel from your hands.

You really lost someone special.

لَّي بيدِإ الباب بِإِيدُه بَدّوه يسمَع الجَواب : مَن يَدُقُ البابَ بيَدِه سيَسْمَعُ الجوابَ

Someone who knocks on the door with his hand will hear the sound.

You asked for it.

دِءْ الحَديد بِإِيدَك وهوِّ حامي : دُقْ الحَديدَ بيَدِكَ وهوَ حامِياً

Knock on the metal with your hands when it is still hot.

Strike while the iron is hot.

الفَقير لّي راسُه مَرْفوعْ أحْسَن من غَني بِإِيدُه كَلَبْشاتْ : الفَقيرُ الذي رَأسُهُ مرْفوعٌ أفْضَلُ مِن غَنِي بيَدِهِ كَلَبْشاتٍ

The poor man with a high head is better than a wealthy man whose hands are in handcuffs.

It is better to be honest and poor than wealthy and in chains.

كُل واحِدْ بِينْلَع شَوْكُه بِإيدُه : كُلُّ واحِدٍ يَقْلَعْ شَوْكَهُ بِيَدِهِ

Each person can pull their thorn in their own hands.

Let everyone deal with their own problems.

إيد من وَرا وإيد من إدّام : يدٌّ من خَلفٍ ويَدٌّ مِن أمامٍ

With one hand in the back and one in the front.

Coming empty handed.

ما تأمِّن لَلغَبِي وبإيده السَيْف : لا تُؤَمِّنْ لِلأحْمَقِ وَبِيَدِهِ السَيْف

Don't trust someone who has a sword in his hands.

ما تعَضّ الإيد لّي بِتطَعْميك : لا تعُضْ اليَدُ التي تُطْعِمُكَ

Don't bite the hand that feeds you.

FOOD AND DRINK

الأكِلْ : الطَعامُ (مُفردات من المطْبَخْ)

الطبْخُ نَفَسٌ : الطبَخ نَفَس

Cooking is spirit.

You can feel the spirit that went into cooking the meal.

نقسِمُ البيْدَر بِالنُّصفِ : منُوَسِمْ البيْدَرْ بِالنْص

Let's cut the field in half.

Let's share.

دُقْ الماءَ بالماءِ : دِءْ الماي بِالماي

Pound on water with water.

That person will never change.

انتَهيْنا بِشُربَةِ ماءٍ : رُحْنا بشُرْبِتْ ماي

We ended like a drink of water.

Misfortune destroyed us.

يبيعُ الماءَ في حيْ السقايين : بِبيع الماي بِحَيْ السآيين

He sells water in the neighborhood of the water sellers.

He manages to succeed even when surrounded by many competitors.

بَصَلْتَك مَحْروءه : بصلتُكَ محروقةٌ

Your onion is burnt.

You are impatient.

صامْ وصامْ وفُطِرِ عَبَصَلي : صامَ وَصامَ ثُمَّ فطرَ على بَصَلةٍ

He fasted and fasted and then had an onion for breakfast.

Describes someone who waits for something and then accepts something less than average.

البَلَد لَّي بتوصلّها كُل مِن بَصَلْها : البَلدُ التي تصلُ لها كُلْ مِنْ بصلِها

Whenever you reach a new country eat an onion right away.

Eat an onion so you do not get sick.

يوم عَسَل يَوم بَصَل هَيْدي الدني : يوْمٌ عسلٌ ويوْمٌ بصلُ هذهِ هيَ الدُنيا

One day honey, another day an onion: this is life.

Life has its ups and downs.

خَلّي العَسَل بِجْرارو حَتى تِجي أسْعارو : أترُكْ العَسَلَ بأجرارهِ حتى يأتي السعرَ المناسِبَ

Leave honey in its jar until it can get a good price.

Wait for a better price (This relates to anything dealing with selling)

كلام كالعَسَل وفعل كالأسَل : كلامٌ كالعَسَلِ وَفعلٌ كالأسلِ

Words like honey and actions like a spike.

Words are different from actions.

يا مؤمِنِه بالرِجّال متل الماي بِالغِرْبال : يا مؤمنةٌ بِالرجالِ مثلَ الماءِ بِالغربالِ

Oh, she who believes in a man! He is like water passing through a colander.

You can't depend on a man.

نحْنا متل السَمِن عَالعَسَلْ : نحنُ مِثلَ السمْنِ على العَسَلِ

We are like butter on honey.

We are like two peas in a pod.

إذا كان حبيبَك عَسَل ما تِلْعَوَ كِلّو : إذا كانَ حبيبُكَ عَسَلاً لا تأكُلْهُ كُلّهُ

If your loved one is like honey don't eat all of him or her.

Don't completely take advantage of your loved one.

أكَل الأخضَر واليابِس : أكَلَ الأخضرَ وَاليابِس (لم يترُك شَيْء لأحَد)

He ate both the fresh and dried vegetables.

He is so greedy. He ate everything and left nothing for anyone else.

حَطَّيْت مِلح عَالجُرِحْ : وضَعْتَ ملحاً على الجُرحِ

To put salt on a wound

To rub salt into the wound.

بيْناتْنا خُبز و ملح : بَيْنَنا خُبزٌ وَملحٌ

We have shared bread and salt.

We can never betray each other and will remain loyal.

خَلّينا نحُط خُبزتي عَجبنْتَك : دعْنا نضَعُ خُبْزَتي على جُبْنَتَكَ

Let me put my bread on your cheese.

Let's share our lives.

عْطي خُبزَك لَلْخبّاز لَوْ أكَل نُصّه : أَعطي خُبْزَك لِلْخبّازِ وَلَو أكَل نِصْفَه

Give your bread to the baker even if he takes half of it.

Deal with a professional, even if you have to pay a lot for it.

الضَيْف أوَّل يَوْم أمَر تاني يوْم رغيف مأَمَر تالِت يوم إرْد مصوَّر : الضّيْفُ أوَّلُ يَوْم قَمَرٌ ثاني يَوْمٍ رَغيفٌ مُقَمَّرٌ ثالِثُ يَوْمٍ قِرْدٌ مُصَوَّرٌ

The first day a guest is like the moon, the second day like a dried piece of bread, and the third day like a monkey.

Guests, like fish, begin to smell after three days.

الجوعْ خُبز الثَوْرَه : الجوعُ خبزُ الثَوْرَةِ

Hunger is the bread of a revolution.

Hunger will ignite the flames of a revolution.

تغدّا و تمدّد تعشّا و تمشّا : تناوَلْ غِذاءَكَ ثُمَّ تَمَدَّدْ وَتَناوَلْ عَشاءَكَ ثُمَّ تمشَّى

After lunch, rest; after dinner, go for a walk.

After lunch you can rest, but make sure you exercise after dinner.

يُطْلَعْ من المولِد من دون حُمُّص : يَطْلَعُ منِ المولِدِ مِنْ دونِ حمُّصٍ

He did not even get a chickpea from the prophet's birthday celebration.

He got absolutely nothing from the situation.

إنتَ متل الزيْتونه ما بِتجي إلاّ بِالرَصْ : أنتَ مثْلُ الزَيْتونَة لا تأتي إلاّ بالرصِ

You are like an olive, you only come once crushed.

You will only obey if you are forced.

ما تحُط كِل البَيْض بِسَلِه وِحْدِه : لا تضعْ كلُّ البيْضِ في سلةٍ واحدةٍ

Don't put all your eggs in one basket.

لّي بياكُل عَضُرْسُه بِيِنْفَعْ نَفْسُه : منْ يأكُلُ على ضرسِهِ ينفَعُ نفْسَه

He who eats with his own teeth serves his own interest.

When you depend on yourself you can best serve your own interest.

تْغَدّا فيه أبِل ما بِتْعَشّى فيكْ : تغذّى فيهِ قبلَ أن يتعشّى فيكَ

Eat him for lunch before he eats you for dinner.

Make sure you defeat him before he defeats you.

زيوان بَلَدَك ولا أمح الغَريب : زيوانُ بلدُكَ وَلا قمحُ الغريبِ

The part of the grain that is not eaten and not the grain of a stranger.

The useless things of your own country are better than the best that strangers can offer.

كولْ عَزوْأك و لْبوس عَزوْء الناس : كُلْ على ذَوْقِكَ وَ ألبُسْ على ذَوْقِ الناسِ

Eat what you want, but dress as others want.

Do the private things that you want, but all public things must consider the opinion of others.

وَرا كُلْ طَبْخا مَحروءة مرا عالفيسبوك : خَلْفَ كُلِ طَبْخة مَحروقَة إمْرَأة على الفيْسْبوك

Behind every burnt dish is a woman on Facebook.

عالمِشمِش : مَثْلَ المُشْمُشْ

Like apricots

Something that will not last, like the apricot season which is short.

ما فيكْ تِجْني مِن الشَوْكْ عِنَبْ : لا تَسْتَطيعْ أن تَقطُفَ مِنَ الشَوْكِ عِنَباً

You cannot get the grapes from the thorns.

Be cautious.

الطَعام نصفهُ يُقيت ونصفَهُ يُميت : الطعامُ نصفُهُ يُشبِعُ ونصفُهُ يُميتُ

Half of the meal fills you up and the other half kills.

Eat in moderation. Over eating is not healthy.

لَيْش عَمتْتَنَفِّخ اللَبَن لأنّو الحَليب كاويني : لماذا تنفُخُ على اللَبَنِ .... لإنّ الحليبَ حرَقَني (حرص زيادة)

Why are you blowing on the yogurt? Because the milk burnt me.

Once bitten, twice shy.

بَدَّك تاكُلْ العِنَبْ أوْ تِنتُل الناطورْ : أتُريدْ أن تأكُلَ العِنَبَ أم تَقْتُلَ الناطورَ

Do you want to eat the grape or kill the guard?

Take things easy. Don't make things more difficult for yourself.

94

دود الخَل منُه وفيه : الدودُ المَوْجودِ في الخَلِ هو مِنْهُ

The worm in the vinegar is a part of it.

The fault is not in our stars, but in ourselves.

عَدَس بِتُرابو وكِل شي بِحْسابو : لِنَتَّفِقَ من البدايةِ ما دامَ العَدَس في التُرابِ

Let's calculate everything while the lentils are in the ground.

Let's come to an agreement at the very beginning before things get complicated.

لَي بْيَعرف بيَعْرِف ولَي ما بيَعْرِف يؤول كَف عَدَس : الذي يَعْرِفُ يَعْرِفُ والذي لا يَعْرِفُ يَقولُ كَفَ عَدَسٍ

He who knows says that he knows. He who does not know says: "a palm of lentils."

(A man caught his daughter in a lentil field with a boy. The boy then ran off with a palm of lentils. When people asked the boy why the girl's father was running after him, he said he had taken a palm of lentils, rather then telling the truth. Used in context when someone does not know the answer to something and just says "palm of lentils")
This is not really truth, but who cares, it's just a palm of lentils.

يا داخِل بَيْن البَصلِه وْإِشْرتا ما إلَكْ إلاّ ريحِتا : يا داخِل بَيْنَ البَصَلة وَقِشْرَتُها لَيْس لكَ إلاّ رائِحَتُها

Oh, you who interfered in the dispute between the onion and its peels.
All that was left for you was the smell.

Refers to someone who interferes in the business of others, and ends up faced with all the trouble.

ANIMALS

امثال مع الحيوانات

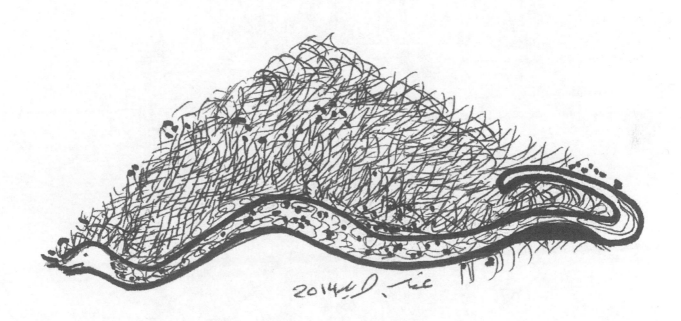

متل الحيِه تَحت التبنِ : مثلَ الحيَّةِ تَحْتَ التبنِ

He is like a snake under the hay.

Like a snake in the grass..

كَلْب الأمير أمير : **كلبُ الأميرِ أميرٌ**

The Prince's dog is a prince.

He who belongs to the prince will also have an opulent life.

جِنِيت عَنَفْسا بَراقِش (مَثَل عِراقي مُسْتَخْدَم في الشّام) : جَنَتْ على نفْسِها براقِش

Baraqesh brought the problems upon himself.

(This is adapted from an Iraqi folklore. There were two tribes fighting with each other. When one tribe came to attack the other, they heard no sounds. Just as the tribe was about to withdraw, the dog Baraqesh began to bark. The noise alerted the tribe that there were people there and they came back and attacked.)

This proverb refers to someone who asks for his own problems.

الكَلْب لّي بيِرْكُض وَرا ذيْلو بيِرْكُض بيِرْكُض وبيِبْأى محلّو :
الكَلْبُ الذي يَرْكُضُ وَراءَ ذَيْلِهِ يرْكُضُ وَيَبْقى مَكانَهُ

The dog that runs and runs after his tail will stay in the same place.

If you run after the impossible, you will remain in the same place.

إجا الديب للغَنَم راح الكَلْب يُخْرا : أَتى الذِئبُ لِلْغَنَم ذَهَبَ الكلبُ يخْرأُ

The wolf approached the sheep, and the guard dog pooped.

When there was a problem, the person who was supposed to help did not bear his responsibility.

لا يْموت الديب ولا بِفْنى الغَنَمْ : لا تَدَعْ الذِئبَ يَموتُ وَلا الغَنَم يَنْقَطِعُ

Don't let the wolf die and the sheep disappear.

Let's be fair and find a middle ground.

لّي ما بيكونْ ديبْ بتاكْله الديابْ : الذي لا يَكونُ ذِئبٌ تَأكُلُهُ الذِئابُ

Someone who is not a wolf will get eaten by a wolf.

The strong trample on the weak.

ذكْر الديبْ و حضَر الأضيب : أذكُر الديبَ وَ حَضَّر القضيبَ (عندما نذكر أحد لا بد أن يأتي)

They mentioned the bear and the hunter came.

Someone came just as we were talking about him.

ذَكَرْنا الأُطّ آمْ الأُطّ : ذَكَرْنا الهِر قامَ الهِر

They mentioned the cat and the cat got up.

Speak of the devil.

متل الأطّة بِسَبعْ أرْواحْ : مثلَ الهِرَّةِ بِسَبعِ أرواحٍ

He is like a cat with seven lives.

He is like a cat with nine lives.

تُضرُب عَصفورَيْن بِحَجَر : تضْرِبُ عصفورَيْن بِحجرٍ

To kill two birds with one stone.

هو مِتِل عصفور طَيّار : هوَ مثلَ عُصفورٍ طَيّارٍ

He is like a free bird.

He is free as a bird..

العُصفور بيِتْقَلَّى والصيّاد بيِتأَلَّى : العصفورُ ينَظِّفُ نَفْسَهُ لِيَصيرَ كالفلِ الأبيضِ والصيّادُ ينتَظِرُ بعصبيّةٍ

The bird is cleaning itself as the hunter is waiting impatiently.

Someone is waiting to do something completely out of reach and thus he is getting frustrated.

الجَمَل ما بيشوف حِرْدَبْتُه : الجمَلُ لا يَرى حردبَّتَهُ

The camel cannot see its own hump.

People cannot see their own faults.

فِرخ البَط عُوّام : فِرْخُ البَطِ يَعومُ كَأهلِهِ

A baby duck is a swimmer.

A chip off the old block.

إنّ الطيور عَأشْكالِها بتوءع : إنَّ الطيورَ على أشكالِها تقعُ

Birds fall upon their same kinds.

Birds of a feather flock together.

الأرايبْ عَءارِب : الأقاربُ عقاربٌ

Relatives are Scorpions (a play on words)

الحمار ما بيوءعْ بالجورة مرتَيْن : الحِمارُ لا يَقَعُ في الجورَةِ مرَّتيْن

The donkey does not fall into the pit twice.

Even an ignorant person does not make the same mistake twice.

ما تشتر حمارَه وإمّها بالحارَه وكِل زِيارَه بزِيارَه : لا تشتَّري حمارةً وأمَها بالحارَةِ وكُلُّ زِيارةً بِزِيارَةٍ

Don't buy a donkey whose mother lives in the same neighborhood or there will be visit after visit.

Don't marry a girl whose mother lives in the neighborhood or your mother-in-law will be visiting you constantly.

أنا أمير وإنْتَ أمير مين بيسوء الحَمير : أنا أميرٌ وإنْتَ أميرٌ مَن سَيَقودُ الحَميرَ

I am a prince and you are a prince, so who will steer the donkey?

We both think we are so great. So who will step down and do the basic things?

حُطّ بالخُرِجْ : ضَعْ في الخُرِجِ

Put it on the donkey's saddle.

Ignore it.

يا آخِد الإرد عَماله راح المال بإي الإرْد عَحالُه : يا آخِذٌ القِرْدَ عَلى مالِهِ راحَ المالُ وَبَقِيَ القِرْدُ على حالِهِ

Oh, you who married a monkey because of his money. Then the money disappeared and the monkey remained.

Referring to someone who married someone who is unattractive for wealth and then when the money disappeared was just left with the unbecoming person.

شو جاب الإرد لإسم أله : ما الذي أتى بالقِرْدِ لإسمِ ألله

Who brought the monkey to the name of God?

What an unfair comparison. Why are you comparing two completely opposite people?

الفِرْخْ الفَصيح مِن البَيْضَه بيصيّح : الفِرْخُ الفَصيْحُ مِنَ البَيْضةِ يَصيْحُ

The smart chick is smart from the time it is in the egg.

Smart people are already intelligent in the womb.

الثُلم الأعْوَج مِن الثَوْر الكَبير : الثُلمُ الأعوَجُ مِنَ الثورِ الكبيرِ

The irrigation ditch is crooked from the bull.

If something is in bad shape, blame the person who was supposed to be responsible.

متل الطاووس : مِثلَ الطاووسِ

Like a peacock

Arrogant

دُموع التماسيح : دموعُ التماسيحِ
Crocodile tears.

غابَ الأُطْ إلْعَب يا فار : غابَ الهِرُ إلْعَبْ يا فأرُ

The cat is gone. Oh, mouse, come and play.

When the cat's away the mice will play.

105

آلو لَلديك صيحْ وْطير آل شَغلتَيْن سَوا ما بيصير : قالوا للديكِ صِحْ وطِرْ فقالَ عَمَلَيْن مَع بَعضٍ لا يَجوزْ

They told the rooster to crow and fly and he responded that it is not wise to do two things at once.

Concentrate on one thing at a time.

بِضْرَب لِحْمار جابولُه الريحان يْشِمُّه آم أكَلُه بتِمُّه : الحِمارُ أعْطوهُ الريحانَ حتّى يَشُمَّهُ قامَ فَأكَلَهُ

Curse the donkey. They brought him basil to smell and he ate it with his mouth.

To cast pearls before swine.

عَرَج الجَمَل مِن شِفْته : عَرَجَ الجَمَلُ مِن شَفَتِهِ

The camel is limping due to its lips.

To make a silly excuse for something, in order to get out of having responsibility.

مِنَ الباب بيْطلَع جَمَل : مِنَ الباب يخرجُ جمَلٌ

A camel is able to leave through this door.

If you are not pleased in this house, the door is wide and you can leave.

الباب بيفَوِّت جَمَل : البابُ يُدْخِل جَمَل

The camel is able to enter through this door.

If you are not pleased in this house, the door is wide and you can leave.

يا ما الجَمَلْ كَسَّر بطِّيخ : كَثيراً ما الجمَلُ كسَّرَ بَطِّيخاً

A watermelon even fell from a camel's back and broke.

It is not a big deal. This kind of mistake can happen to anyone.

دنَب الكَلب أعْوَج ولَوْ حَطَّيْتُه بالآلِب أربعين سنِه : ذنَبُ الكَلبِ لَوْ بقِيَ في القالِبِ أرْبَعينَ سنةً يظَلُ أعْوَجاً

If a dog's tail stayed in a mold for forty years, it would still come out crooked.

As much as you try, he will not change.

107

الحَمير حَمير لَوْ لِبْسِت حَرير : الحميرُ تبقى حميرٌ حتى لو لبِستْ حريراً

The donkey is a donkey even if it wears silk.

The ignorant one is ignorant no matter how he tries to embellish himself.

COLORS
ألْوان

تَبييض الأمْوال : **تبييضُ الأموالِ**

Whitening money

Money laundering

أله يبيِّض حَظُّه فيه : **أللهُ يُبيِّضُ حظَّهُ فيهِ**

May God whiten your luck because of him.

May your friendship with this person bring you luck from God.

حصان أبْيَض : **حِصانٌ أبيضٌ**

A white horse

Prince charming

أله يُبيِّض بَخْته و يِبْعَتْله بنْت حَلال : **أللهُ يِبيِّضُ بخّتَهُ ويَبعثُ لهُ إبنةً حلالٍ**

God whiten his luck and send him a good girl

May fortune shine upon him and send him a good girl.

بِبيِّض صَفِحْتُه : **يُبيِّضُ صفحتَهُ**

He is whitening his pages.

He wants to start all over (turn a new page).

يا خبَر أبيضْ : يا خبرٌ أبيَضٌ

Oh, white news!

Great news!

كِذبِه بَيْضا : كِذبَةٌ بيضاءٌ

A white lie!

نْفوت عَبَياض و نُضهر عَبَياض : نَدخُلُ على بياضٍ ونخرُجُ على بياضٍ

Start on white and end on white.

Let everything be clear from the beginning in order to end clearly.

حتّى الجنْ الأزرَأ ما بيَعرِف : حتى الجنَّ الأزرقُ لا يعرفُ

Even the green devil does not know.

No one knows where it is.

نَفسُه خَضْرا : نفسُهُ خُضراءٌ

He wants green.

An old man who likes young women.

يا نْهار أسْوَد : يا نهارٌ أسودٌ

What a black day!

What a bad day

بَعْد الكَبْرَه جِبِّه حَمْرا : بعدَ الكبرةِ جبَّةٌ حَمْراءٌ

Refers to someone who wears red in his or her old age.

Refers to an elderly person with the sudden urge to marry: people will say that now suddenly he or she wants to wear a bright red dress, something inappropriate at his or her old age.

يا خَبَر أسْوَد : يا خبرٌ أسودٌ

What black news!

What bad news!

خبّي إرشَك الأبيضْ لَلْيوْم الأسْوَد : خَبِّئ قِرْشَكَ الأبيَضَ ليومِكَ الأسوَد

Hide your white money for a black day.

Save your money for a time when you are really in need.

مو كِل شي بيِلْمَع دهَب : لَيْس كُلُ ما يَلْمَعُ ذهَبٌ

Not everything that shines is really gold.

All that glitters is not gold.

الكَلاَمْ مِنْ فِضّة وَالسُكوت مِنْ ذَهَبْ : الكَلامُ مِنْ فضةٍ والسكوتُ مِنْ ذَهبٍ

Words are silver and silence is gold.

Silence is better than talking (Silence is golden).

الوَئت مِن ذهَبْ : الوقتُ منْ ذهبٍ

Time is gold.

The Home
البَيْت

لَي بَدُّه يَعْمِل جِمّال بيعَلّي باب بيتُه : الذي يُريدُ أن يعْمَلَ جَمَالاً يُعَلّي بابَ بَيْتِه

He who wants to do good should start at the door of his own home.

Charity begins at home.

بَسْ بِجي الصَبي مِنْصَلّي عَالنَبي : عِنْدَما يَأتي الصَبي نُصَلّي على النَبي

Let the baby boy arrive and then we'll pray to the prophet.

Let the great event and then we will talk about it.

ما أعَزْ مِن الوَلَد إلاّ وَلَد الوَلَد : ليسَ أعزُ مِنَ الولدِ إلا ولد الولدِ (الحَفيد)

There is nothing dearer than the child of your child.

Your grandchild is even more precious than your own child.

الرِجّال بالبيْت نِعْمِه حتّى لَو فَحْمِه : الرجلُ في البيْتِ نعمةٌ حتى ولَوْ كانَ فحمةً

A man in the house is a blessing even if he is just like a lump of coal

Better to have a man in the house even if he is useless.

حَنون البَيْت نورْ البَيْت : حنونُ البيْتِ نورُ البيت

The warmth of the house is the light of the house.

A nice person can light up a house.

البيْت بَلا حرْمِه بيصير خِرْبِه : البيْتُ مِن دونِ إمْرأةٍ يَصيرُ خَراباً

A house with no woman will be in ruins.

البيْت منوَّر بِأصْحابِه : البيْتُ منوَّرٌ بِأصْحابِهِ

The house is lit by its inhabitants.

The inhabitants define the warmth of the house.

هَمَّ البَنات لِلمَماتْ : هَمُّ البناتِ حتى المَوْتِ

Concern about girls lasts until death.

Daughters bring great concern to their families all their lives.

بنْت منيحة وَلا صَبي فَضيحَة : بنتٌ منيحةٌ ولا صبيٌ فضيحةٌ

Better a nice daughter rather than a scandalous son.

الرجَال جَنّى والمَرا بَنَّا : الرَجُلُ يَجني (يُدَخِّل) والمَرأةُ تبْني

A man brings in and a woman builds the home.

A man brings in the income and the woman provides the foundation of the home.

يا رايِحْ عَالجَبَل جيبْ لأهْلَك وَلو حَجَر : يا ذاهِبْ على الجَبَل قَدِّمْ لأهْلَك وَلَوْ حَجَراً

If you are going to the mountains, bring back something for your family even if just a stone.

Refers to returning from a trip with gifts for your family.

طُبّ الجرّة عَتِمّا بتطلع البنت لأمّا : أقُلُبْ الجَرَّةَ عَلى فَمِها فتُصْبِحُ الفَتاةَ مِثلَ أُمِّها

Turn the jar over and the daughter will turn out like her mother.

See, she turned out exactly like her mom! (in a negative sense).

إبن الحَلال عِنْدَ ذِكْرِه يْبان : إِبْنُ الحَلالِ عِنْدَ ذِكْرِهِ يَظهَرُ

The honorable son appears when he is remembered.

This proverb is used when someone appears before you just as you are speaking kindly about them.

إن كِبِر إبنك خاويه : إِن كَبُرَ إِبْنَكَ عامِلْهُ كأخيكَ

When your son grows up treat him like your brother.

Stop ruling over him; he is equal to you.

الوَلَدْ سِر أبيه (مثل) : الولدُ مثلَ أبيهِ

The son is the secret of his father.

Like father like son

لا يحْمِل هَمَكْ غَيْر إبن بَيَّك وإمَّكْ : لا يحملُ همَكَ غيْرَ أبيكَ وأمكَ

No one carries your concern other than the son of your father and mother.

You can depend on your brother more than anyone else to help you carry your burden.

كونو إخْوي وأسُمو أُسِمة الحَا : كونوا أخوةً وأقْسِموا قُسْمَةَ الحَقِ

Be like brothers and divide evenly among yourselves.

Be fair.

أنا وخَيي عَابن عَمّي وأنا وإبن عَمّي عَالغَريب : أنا وَأخي ضِدَ إِبنُ عَمّي وَأنا وَإِبنُ عَمّي ضِدَ الغَريبِ

My brother and I against my cousin, and my cousin and I against a stranger

This proverb speaks to the importance of family.

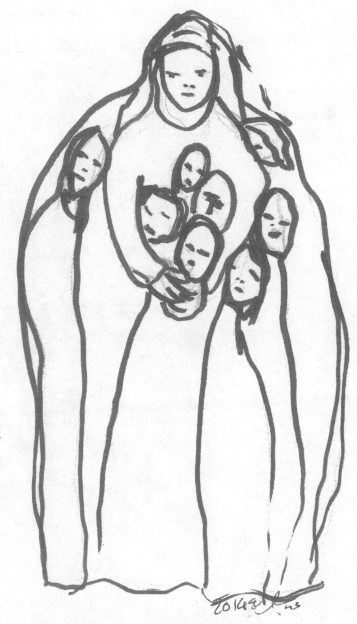

الأم بِتْلِم : الأُمُ تَجْمَعُ (عائلتها)

A woman gathers.

A woman is the one who brings the family together.

HOSPITALITY

الضيافِه : الضِيافَة

حَماتِك بِتْحِبّك : حماتُكِ تحبُكِ

Your mother-in-law loves you.

Welcome, you've come at the right time, we're about to eat.

لاءِيني وما تطَعْميني : لاقيني وَلا تُطعِمْني

Don't feed me; receive me well.

Better to be kind and welcoming to me than lavish food upon me in a cold way.

ما غَريب إلا الشيطان : ليسَ غَريبٌ إلا الشيطان

No one is a stranger except the devil.

Don't feel you are just a guest, for you are one of us.

إذا بدَّك تالِعْ ضَيْفَك كَنِّس بَيْتَك : إذا أرَدتَ أن تقلَعَ ضَيْفَك كَنِّسْ بَيْتَك

If you want to kick out your guest, start to clean your house.

بَيْت الضيء بيساع ألفْ صَديء : البيْت الضَيِّق يَسَعْ ألفْ صَديق

A cramped house fits a thousand friends.

You should be generous and make enough room for all your guests.

MARRIAGE
الزواج

الحُبّ سَتَّار العُيوب : الحبُ يستُر العيوب

Love covers faults.

وَرا كل رِجّال عَظيم مَرا : وَراءَ كُلُ رَجُل عَظيم إمرأةً

Behind every successful man is a woman.

لَّي ما بِتْخاف مِنْه مَرْتُه مَنُّه زَلْمه : من لا تخافُ منهُ إمرأتَهُ لا يكونُ رجلاً

He who is not afraid of his wife is not a man.

الرِجّال بيترَبّا مَرتَيْن عِنْد أهْله و عِنْد مَرْتُه : الرجلُ يتربى مرتين عندَ أهلِهِ وعندَ إمرأتِهِ

A man is raised twice: once in his family's house and once at his wife's house.

المَرا بِتترَبا تلات مَرّات عِنْد أهلا وجَوْزا ووْلادا :
الإمْرأةُ تتربّى ثلاثَ مَرّاتٍ في بَيْتِ أهْلِها وَزَوْجِها ومَعْ أوْلادِها

A woman is raised three times: once in her family's house, with her husband, and then with her children.

يَلّي بدُّه يْعيش عيشَه هَنِيّه ياخُد وحِده شامِيّه : الذي يُريدُ أن يعيشَ عيشةً هنيّةً يأخذُ إمرأةً شاميّةً

He who wants to live a warm and blessed life should marry a Damascene woman.

الزَواج متل البَطّيخة يا حمرا يا بَيْضا : الزَواجُ كالبطيخةِ إمّا أحمَر أو أبيَضْ

Marriage is like a watermelon. It can turn out either red or white.

The way marriage turns out is all about luck.

متل الأطْرَشْ بِالزَفَّه : مثلَ الأطْرَشِ في حَفْلَةِ الزفاف

He is like the deaf at a wedding ceremony.

He has absolutely no idea what is going on.

أذْما يْكون الرجّال عاءِل ما بيْندر عَحيلِت المرا : مَهْما يَكونُ الرجُلُ عاقِلاً لا يَقْدِرُ على حيلَةِ المرأة

As smart as the man is he will not be able to contend with the cunning of a woman.

إمْشي بِجَنازتُه ولا تِمْشي بِزَواجُه : إمْشي بجنازتِهِ ولا تمشي بزواجِهِ

Walk at his funeral but not at his wedding.

So much will he suffer in his marriage that it is better to attend his funeral than his marriage celebration.

الحُبْ أعْمى : الحبُ أعمى

Love is blind.

الضُرَّه مُرّه : الضرّةُ مرَّةٌ

A co-wife is bitter.

Polygamy is a hard thing to have to deal with.

أوّل مَرا مُراتي وْتاني مَرا ياحَياتي : أوَّلُ إمرأة ... إمْرأتي وتاني إمْرأة ....يا حَياتي (الزَوْجة)

The first woman he just called a wife, but the second wife he calls his life.

The second marriage is better.

NEIGHBOR

الجارْ

الجارْ وَلَوْ جارْ : الجارُ وَلَوْ أساءَ إلَيْكَ

The neighbor even if a neighbor.

He is still a neighbor after all even if he has hurt you. This is about the importance of the neighbor.

الجار أبْل الدار : الجارُ قبْلَ الدارِ

The neighbor before the house

Neighbors are extremely important. Think of who your neighbors are before you get the house.

مين أدرى بِحالَك رَبّك أو جارَك؟ : منْ يدري بحالِكَ ربُّكَ أو جارُكَ؟

Who knows how you are doing, God or your neighbor?

This proverb attests to the importance of your neighbor who knows all about you,
and thus may even be closer to you than God.

الجار الأريب ولا الخَيْ البعيد : الجارُ القَريبُ وَلا الأخُ البَعيدُ

The close neighbor and not the faraway brother.

A close neighbor can be more helpful in your life than a brother who is far away from you.

بحاكيكي يا كِنّه .... اسمَعي يا جاره : أكلِّمُكِ يا كَنَّتي كي تَسْمَعي يا جارة

I am speaking to you, oh daughter-in-law, in order for the neighbor to hear.

When you are trying to send a message to someone by speaking loudly to someone else.

FRIENDSHIP

الصداءة : الصداقة

عَدو عائل أحسَنْ مِن صديء جاهِل : عَدوٌّ عاقِلٌ أفضَل مِن صَديقٍ جاهِلٍ

A smart enemy is better than an ignorant friend.

An incapable friend is more dangerous than any enemy.

إذا كان حَبيبَكْ عَسَل ما تِلْحَسو كِلّو : إذا كانَ حَبيبُكَ عَسَلاً لا تَلْحَسْهُ كُلَّهُ

Even if your loved one is like honey don't devour all of him or her.

Don't take advantage of your loved ones.

الناسْ لَبَعْضا : الناسُ لِبعضِها

People are for each other.

People should help and take care of each other.

ما بيحِنّ عَالعود إلاَّ إشْرو : لا يَحُنُّ على العودِ إلاَّ قَشْرُهُ

It is only the cover that longs for the Oud (musical instrument).

No one feels for you more than those close to you.

جَنِّه بلا ناس ما بتِنْداس : جنّةٌ بِدونِ ناسٍ لا تنداس

A heaven without people is not worth it.

Even if a place is beautiful, if there are no people it is not worth it.

الصَديءْ لَوَءتِ الضـيـء : الصَديقُ لِوَقتِ الضيقِ

A friend is for hard times.

A friend in need is a friend indeed.

لَي شافْ أَحْبابُه نِسِي أَصْحابُه : مَن رأى أَحْبابَهُ نَسِيَ أَصْحابَهُ

He saw a beloved friend and forgot all the others.

He is now dealing just with the new person and has forgotten his other friends.

صَديئك لَي بِبَكِّيك مو لَي بِجامْلَك : صديقُكَ هو الذي يبكيكَ وليس الذي يُجامِلُكَ

Your true friend is the one who makes you cry not the one who pays you false compliments.

كِتْرِت الأَعْتابْ بِتْفَرِّءُ الأصحاب : كثرتْ الأعتابُ تفرِّقُ الأصحابَ

If you keep on criticizing and complaining, you will find your friends far away.

الرَفيء أبل الَطريء : الرَفيقُ قَبْلَ الطَريقُ

The friend before your life path.

Your choice of friend is more important than even your life path, for good friends will influence you correctly.

بوَأت الضيـء الناس لَبَعْضا : بوقتِ الضيقِ الناسُ لِبَعْضِها

During hard times people help each other.

لا يَصْلُحْ رَفِيقاً مَن لا يَبْتَلِعْ رِيقاً : لا يَنْفَعْ أن يَكونَ صَديقاً لَكَ مَنْ لا يَعْرِفْ أن يَسْكُتَ

You cannot be a friend to someone who can't swallow their own saliva.

Don't be friends with someone who talks too much and is never quiet.

لازِم تعاشْرُه تا تَعِرْفُه : يَجِبُ أن تَتَعَامَلَ مَعَهُ حتَّى تتعَرَّفَ إلَيْه

You need to deal with him in order to get to know him.

لي ساواك بِنَفْسُه ما ظَلَمَك : مَن عامَلَك كما يُعامِلُ نَفْسَهُ لَمْ يَظْلِمْك

Someone who treats you the way he treats himself will not oppress you.

If someone treats you the way he treats himself don't take offense even if you are not entirely happy with the way you are treated.

127

DESTINY

النصيب

الطينه مو للعَجينَه : الطِينَةُ لَيْسَتْ لِلعجينَةِ

The clay is not for the dough.

The two of them are not meant for each other.

إذا بِتِرْكُض رَكَض الوحوش غَيْر رِزأك ما بِتحوش : إِذا ركضْتَ ركُضَ الوحوشِ غَيْرَ رزقَكَ لا تجمعْ

Even if you run like a wild animal you will still only gain that which was meant to be yours.

No matter how hard you work you will only get what was destined to be yours.

الزَواج أسِمه و نَصيب : الزَواجُ قُسْمَةٌ وَ نَصيبٌ

Marriage is destiny.

You will marry he whom you are destined for.

ما يْصيبَك إلا نَصيبَك : لا يُصيبُكَ غيْر نصيبكَ

You only get that which you are destined for.

الحَذَر لا يمْنَع القَدَر : الحذرُ لا يمنَعْ القدرَ

Caution won't ward off destiny.

It is good to be cautious in life, but destiny still counts.

المَكْتوبْ ما مِنّو مَهْروبْ : ليسَ منَ المُمْكِنِ أن نَهْرُبَ مِنَ الشَيْءِ المَكْتوبِ

You cannot escape that which is written.

Che sarà, sarà.

WORK

الشغل

مِن الفَرْشه لِلوَرشه : مِنَ الفرشةِ لِلوَرشةِ

From the bed to the studio.

All he does is sleep and work.

يِتمَسْكَن حتّى يِتْمَكَّن : يتمسكنُ حتى يتمكَّنُ

To make oneself look weak before positioning oneself

Describes someone who acts very weak and vulnerable before establishing his position and then showing his true character.

لّي أوَّلُه شَرط آخِرتُه نور : الذي أوَّلُهُ شرطٌ آخِرتَهُ نورٌ

When the condition is made at the commencement, the end is light.

When the agreement is clear from the beginning, the end results will be positive.

شَرْط عَالحَألِه ولا أتال عَالبَيْدَر : شرطٌ على الحقلةِ ولا قتالٌ على البيدرِ

Put the conditions in the field and then you won't fight over the harvested field grains.

Make all things clear from the beginning of the agreement in order to avoid fighting later on.

العُمر بيُخْلَص والشُغِل ما بيُخْلَص : العمرُ ينتهي والشغلُ لا ينتهي

Life ends but work does not.

Take a break. There will always be enough work to last a lifetime. Your life will end before all your work does.

مال الحَرام متل ما بيجي بيروحْ : مالُ الحَرامِ مثلَ ما يأتي يَذهَب

Stolen money goes as easily as it came.

Money that is not honestly hard-earned will not last.

الطيز النّآلي مو شِغالِه : الإنْسانُ الذي يُغيّرُ أشْغالَهُ ليسَ صالِحٌ للشُغلِ

The buttock that changes places all the time is not working.

A person who keeps changing his job won't contribute well to his tasks.

بيْكونْ عَمبِؤصْ الشَعِر بيصير عَمْبِيأبَعْ ضراس : بيْنما كانَ يقصُ الشعرَ أصبحَ يُقبّعُ اضراساً

He was a barber and then he became a dentist.

A person who goes from one thing to another without ever completing a task.

ما أحْلى الشِدِّي لّي بَعْدا الفَرَج : ما أحْلى الشِدةَ التي بَعْدَها الفَرَج

How nice is hard work that is followed by joy.

How nice it is to work hard at something when the end result is something wonderful.

ما تأجّل عَمَل اليَوْم لَغَد : لا تُؤَجِّلْ عَمَلَ اليَوْمَ إلى الغَدِ

Don't put off today's work until tomorrow.

لَي طلب العُلى بيسْهر الليالي : مَن طَلَبَ العُلى سَهِرَ اللَيالي

If someone wants to ask for something important he has to stay up late.

You have to work hard for it.

لَي بيجد بيوجد : مَنْ جَدَّ وَجَدَ

He who worked seriously found it.

If you work hard you get what you want.

مِتِل ما بِتزرعْ بتُحْصُدْ : كما تَزْرعُ تَحْصُدُ

You will reap the harvest of that which you plant.

You reap what you sow.

الإسْكافي حافي والحايِك عُريان : الإسْكافي من دونِ حِذاءٍ والحايِك من دونِ ثِيابٍ

The shoemaker is barefoot and dress maker is naked.

The shoemaker's children go barefoot.

باب النجّار مَكْسور و مَرْت السكّاف حافيِه : بابُ النجّارِ مَكسورٌ وَإمرَأةُ السكّافِ حافِيَةٌ

The carpenter's door is broken and shoemaker's wife is barefoot.

The person who specializes in a profession does not necessarily give benefits to those around him. For example, just because the father or mother is a doctor does not mean they will ensure that their child is healthy.

مطْرَحْ ما بْتِرْزُا إلزؤ : المَكانُ الذي تُرزَقُ فيهِ إلصَقْ بِهِ

Stick to the place where you are able to make a good living.

رَبْنا بِؤولْ أوم تَؤومْ مَعَك مو نام تَأْطْعَمَكْ : رَبُّنا يَقولُ قُمْ لأقومَ مَعَك ليَس نمْ كَيْ أُطْعِمَكَ

Our God says, "Get up and I will get up with you." He does not say sleep, and I will feed you.

God helps those who help themselves.

لَّي ما بياكُل بِايده ما بِيشْبَعْ : الذي لا يأكُلُ بِيَدِهِ لا يَشْبَعْ

He who does not eat from his own hands will not be satisfied.

When you reap the benefits of your own labor you are satisfied.

HOMELAND

الوطن

حُبّ الوَطَن مِن الإيمان : **حُبُّ الوَطَنِ مِنَ الإيمانِ**

Loving the homeland is a religious dictate.

كُل شي فْرَنْجي بْرَنْجي (تُرْكي مُسْتَخْدَم في الشام) : **كلُّ شيءٍ فرنجيٌّ برَنْجيٌّ**

Everything faranji is baranji. (adapted from Turkish)

Everything from the outside is better than what is in our own country. (This is in the negative sense. It refers to someone who has a complex that everything from the outside world is better than that which he can find in his own country.)

الدين لِله وِالوَطَن لِلجَميع : **الدينُ لإله وَالوَطَنُ لِلْجَميعِ**

Religion is for God and the homeland belongs to everyone.

لّي يِزْرَع في غَيْر بَلَدة لا لهْ وَلا لِوَلَدة : **الذي يَزْرَعُ في غَيْرِ بَلَدِهِ لا لَهُ وَلا لِوَلَدِهِ**

That which he plants not in his own country does not belong to him or his son.

مين طِلعْ مِن دارُه ألْ مِنْدارُه : **مَن يَتْرُك دارَهْ يَقِل مِقدارَهُ**

He who leaves his home (homeland) loses all value.

You lose all your sense of value when you leave your homeland.

KNOWLEDGE
العِلمُ

العِلمُ أفْضَلُ من المالْ : العِلمُ أفضَلُ منَ المالِ

Knowledge is more important than money.

الجاهِلُ عَدو نَفْسُه : الجاهِلُ عدوُّ نفسه

Ignorance is its own enemy.

الناس أعْداء ما جَهَلوا : الناسُ أعْداءٌ لِكُلِ ما يجْهَلونَهُ

People are hostile to all they are ignorant of.

People are wary of that which they do not know.

اطلبوا العِلمِ وَلَو بالصين : أطلبوا العِلمَ حتى وَلَو كانَ في الصينِ

Ask for knowledge even if it comes from somewhere as faraway as China.

Refers to the importance of knowledge

ما حَداً بيِخْلأ مَعَلَّم : لا أحَدَّ يولَدُ وَهوَ مُتَعَلِّمٌ

No one is born with knowledge.

عَلَّمْناهون عَلشحادِه سَبَوُونا عَالبواب : عَلَّمناهُم على الشّحادَةِ سَبَقونا على الأبوابِ

We taught them how to beg and they beat us to the door.

We taught them how to do something and they became even more qualified than we are.

آفة العِلْم النسْيان : مصيبَةُ العِلم هي النِسْيانُ

The catastrophe of knowledge is oblivion.

It is a catastrophe that we can forget what we have learned.

لَّي عَلَّمني حَرفْ صُرْت لإله عَبْدْ : مَنْ عَلَّمَني حَرْفاً صِرْتُ لَهُ عَبْداً

I am slave to he who taught me just one letter.

Refers to the importance of attaining knowledge.

العِلْم بالصِغَر متل النَأش عَالحَجَر : العِلْمُ في الصِغَرِ كالنَقْشِ على الحَجَرِ

Attaining knowledge in one's youth is like a carving in a stone.

That which we learn during our youth will stay with us forever.

HUMILITY
التواضع

حُب الذات أصْل العَلّات : مَحَبَّةُ الذاتِ أصلُ الشَر

Narcissism is the basis of all evil.

Conceit is the root of all evil.

الطاسي الفاضي بِترنْ : الوعاءُ الفارِغُ يَرُنُّ

The empty metal vase rings.

An arrogant person is empty inside.

مَن مَدَحَ نَفْسَهُ فهِمَ الناس عَكْسَهُ : الذي يمْدَحُ نفسَه يفْهمُ الناسُ عكْسَهُ

People will interpret the opposite of he who extols himself.

Arrogance is the sign of insecurity.

ألّل كَلامَك يُحْمَد مَآمَك : قَلّلْ كلامَك يُحْمَدُ مَقامُك

Little talk reveals your importance.

An important person does not brag but is quiet about his accomplishments.

السِنِبْلي المَلاني مِنْحنِيّة : السُنْبُلةُ المِلآنةُ تَنْحَني

The full wheat grain bends down.

A person with important qualities is humble.

SATISFACTION

الأناعه : القناعة

القناعة كَنز لا يَفنى : القناعةُ كنزٌ لا يفنى

Satisfaction is a treasure that does not go away.

To be satisfied is an everlasting, invaluable treasure in one's life.

فَلاَّحْ مِكْفِي سُلْطان مِخْفي : فلاَّحٌ مكفيٌّ سلطانٌ مخفيٌّ

A satisfied farmer is a hidden Sultan.

It is as if he is a sultan.

خَيْرُ الغِنى الأنْوع وَشرِّ الفُقَر الخُضوعْ : خَيْرُ الغِنى القُنوعُ وشرُّ الفقرِ الخضوعُ

A blessing that can come from riches is satisfaction and the evil that can come from poverty is subservience.

People with riches can be blessed with satisfaction, and those in poverty can be cursed with subservience.

مو شِبْعان اللِئمِه بِبيْت أهْله : ليْسَ شبْعانُ اللقمةَ في بيْتِ أهلِهِ

He is not satisfied from the bite he had at his parent's house.

Someone who is unsatisfied and still wants more, an opportunist (in a negative sense)

شِبْعان من حَليب إمّه : شَبْعانٌ مِنْ حَليبِ أمّهِ

He is satisfied from his mother's milk.

Describes someone who is content

المَرَه المَكْفِيّه مَلِكه مَخْفِيه : الإمْرَأةُ المَكْفِيّةُ مَلِكَةٌ مَخْفِيّةٌ

A satisfied woman is like a queen.

A woman who is satisfied with her life lives as if she is royalty.

FORGIVENESS
الغِفران : الغُفران

العَفو عِنْد المَأدِرة فَضيلة : العَفو عِنْدَ المَقْدِرة فَضيلةٌ

Forgiveness from a capable individual is nobility.

Even if you are hurt, you can forgive.

ما بْحُط شي بِألبي : لاأضَعُ شَيئاً في قَلْبي

I don't put anything in my heart.

I don't hold grudges

GENEROSITY
الكَرَم

الكَريمْ دايْماً مُسامِحْ : الكريمُ هوَ دائماً مسامحٌ

A generous person is always forgiving

لا جودْ إلاّ مِن المَوْجودْ : لا عطاءٌ إلا مِنَ المَوْجودِ

There should be no generosity but from that which we have.

We must only give what we have.

الكَرَم ستَّار العيوب : الكرمُ يسترُ العيوبَ

Generosity hides faults.

Someone who is generous can use this generosity to cover his faults.

كِل شي إلا البِخِل : كُلُ شَيءٍ إلاّ البُخل

Everything is acceptable but stinginess.

عْمُل خَيْر وارْمي بالبَحِر: إعمَلْ خَيْر وارميه في البَحرِ

Do charity and then throw it in the water.

Do good and then don't talk about it.

EXPERIENCE

تجرِبِه : التجربَة

تيتي تيتي متل ما رُحْتي جيتي : تيتي تيتي كما ذهبْتَ عُدْتَ

Ti ti ti ti as you left you came back

Someone who has an experience but comes back the same

ألف ألْبي ولا غَلْبي : ألف قَلْبَة وَلا غَلَبَة

He has gone through a thousand changes and movements, but has not once been subdued.

ما كِل مَرَّه بتِسْلَم الجَرَّه : لَيْسَ كُلُ مَرَّةً تَسْلَمُ الجَرَّة

The jar is not safe every time.

Don't be overconfident. It may not work next time.

شيل عَاد حَجمَك : أحمُلْ على قدَرِ حجمكِ

He is carrying as much as his body size.

Only take on what you can actually do – according to your means.

لَي بتَعرِفُه أحْلى مِن لَي بتِتْعَرَّف عليْه : الذي تَعرِفَهُ أفضل مِنَ الذي تتعرَّفُ عليْه

That which you know is better than what you get to know.

غَلْطِة الشاطِر بِألِف : غلطةُ الشاطِرُ بِألِفٍ

The smart one made a thousand-fold mistake.

To make a mistake that has dreadful consequences that last a lifetime

لَّي بِيِستِحي بْتُروح علَيْه : مَن يسْتَحي يخْسَرُ

The shy one loses.

If you are too shy and embarrassed you will lose the opportunity for advancement.

لَّي أكْبَر مِنَّك بيَوْم أفْهَم مِنَّك بِسِنِه : مَن هُوَ أكبرُ منكَ بيوْمٍ أفهمُ منكَ بِسنَةٍ

He who is older than you by one day knows more than you by one year.

Age brings wisdom.

إسْأل المْجَرَّب وما تِسْأل الحَكيم : إسْألْ المُجَرَّبَ ولا تَسْألْ الحَكيمَ

Ask the experienced individual and not the wise one.

The person who has experienced this before is even wiser than the one who is supposedly wise.

لَكِل جديدْ رَهْجي ولا كِلْ أديمْ دَفْشي : لِكُلِّ جَديدٍ رَهْجَة ولِكُلِّ قَديمٍ دَفْشَة

Everything new brings excitement and everything old brings boredom.

عِنْدَ الإمْتِحان يُكرَمُ المَرْء أو يُهانْ : عِنْدَ الإمْتِحانُ يُكرمُ المرءُ أو يُهانُ

When an individual is tested he either succeeds or fails.

أَلّل البَرَمان و كَتّر السؤال : قَلّلْ البحثَ وَأكثِرْ منِ السؤالِ

Less searching, more questions.

The more questions you ask, the less you will wander around lost.

في التأنّي السَلامَة وفي العَجَلة النَدامَة : في التأنّي السلامةَ وفي العجَلةِ النَدامةَ

Going slow brings soundness and rushing brings regrets.

It is better to go slowly than to be rushed and filled with regret.

عِشْنا وشِفنا : عِشْنا وَرَأيْنا

We have lived and seen.

We have lived and thus have seen all sorts of things and gained wisdom from them.

عيش كْتير بِتْشوف كْتير : الذي يَعيشُ كثيراً يَرى كَثيراً

Someone who has lived a lot has seen a lot.

Someone who has lived a long time has had many experiences that have allowed him see all sorts of good and bad things.

لّي بيْغيب بتّروحْ عْلَيْه : مَن يَغيبُ يُضَيّعُ الفُرصةَ

The absent one loses the opportunity.

عاشِر الأوْمْ أربعين يَوْم إن ما صُرت منهُم إرْحَل عَنْهُمْ :
عاشِرْ القَوْمَ أربعينَ يَوْماً إن ما صِرْتَ منْهُم إرْحَلْ عنْهُم

Stay with people forty days and if you can't become like them, leave.

If you can't adapt to the people you are with, then leave them.

لَو بدّا تشْتَي غَيَّمِت : إذا أرادَتْ أن تُمطِرَ فسَتُغَيِّمُ

If it was going to rain, the clouds would have been here.

If you were going to do something you would have already started it.

لّي فات مات : ما فاتَ ماتَ

What has passed has died.

It has already happened. Just forget about it.

لكُل حَدَث حَديث : لِكُلِّ حدثٍ حديث

For every happening there is talk.

Let this pass and we can talk about it later.

الأعْمال بِخْواتِمْها : الأعمالُ بخَواتِمِها

The results of work are seen in its conclusion.

The conclusion will show whether it was worth it.

ما بتَعْرِف خَيْري حَتّى تجَرِّب غَيْري : لا تَعْرِفْ خَيْري إلاّ بَعْدَ أن تُجَرِّبَ غَيْري

You will not appreciate how nice I am until you have had experiences with others.

أكَلْ عَلَيْ الدَهرِ وْشرِب : أكَلَ عَلَيْهِ الزَمَنُ وشَرِبَ

Something that has been eaten and drunk by time.

It can be used for someone who has many experiences in life and knows a lot, and can also be used in the negative sense. It depends on the context.

146

HYPOCRISY AND DECEIT

النفاء : النفاق= الكذب

مَوَّتُه و مِشي بِجنازتُه : قتلَهُ ومشى في جنازتِهِ

He killed him and then walked at his funeral.

Describes someone who hurts another person so much but has no decency, and would even pretend to care in front of other people.

حَبْل الكِذِب أصير : حبلُ الكذبِ قصيرٌ

The rope of the lie is short.

The lie will soon be revealed.

الوَرْدِه مْخَبِّيه شَوْكا : الوردةُ مخبِّأةٌ شوْكاً

The flower hides thorns.

Behind something beautiful is that which can cause pain.

حاميها حَراميها : حاميها هوَ حَراميها

Her protector is her thief.

Beware of someone you may trust.

ضَرَبْني و بَكى سَبَأني وِشْتَكى : ضربَني وَبكى سبَقَني واشتَكى

He hit me and cried. He was the one who complained about me.

Describes someone who hurts you and then complains as if you were the one who hurt him.

إتَّقي شَرْ مَن أَحْسَنْتَ إلَيْه : إتَّقي مِن شرِّ مَنْ أحسنتَ إليْه

Beware of evil from those to whom you have done good.

اِلْحاء الكذّاب لَباب بيتُه : إلحَقْ الكَذّابَ إلى بابِ بَيْتِهِ

Follow the liar to the door of his house.

Let's see where this lie will take us.

GOSSIP
الثَرثَرة

الرَسول شايِفْ بِعيونُه وسَتَرْ : الرَسولُ رأى بِعيونِهِ وَسَتَرَ

The Prophet saw the sinner with his own eyes and protected him.

Don't gossip and judge others harshly.

الفَضيحَه إلا ريحَه : الفَضيحةُ لها رائحةٌ

Scandals have their own smell.

A scandal can be sensed from afar.

ما في دِخّان بَلا نار : ليسَ مِنْ دخانٌ بلا نار

There is no smoke without fire.

If people are gossiping there must be something behind the story.

مِنْ هَوْن حَبِّه ومِنْ هَوْن حَبِّه بْيَعِملو عَالبَيْدَر إبِّه : مِن هُنا حَبَّة وَمِنْ هُنا حَبَّة يَعملوا عَلى البَيْدَرِ قُبَّة

Grain from here and grain from there makes a pile of grains in the field.

Too much gossip causes a lot of problems.

لّي بَيْته من أزاز ما بيرْمي الناس بِالحجاره : الذي بَيْتُهُ مِن زُجاجٍ لا يَرْمي الناسَ بِالحِجارةِ

If your house is made of glass, don't throw stones on people.

Don't speak badly of someone if they could also say the same thing of you.

SECRETS

سِر : السِر

ما تِنْشُر غَسيلَك إدّام الناسْ : لا تِنْشُرُ غَسيلَكَ أمامَ الناسِ

Don't hang out your dirty clothes for all to see.

Don't air your dirty laundry.

السِرْ بَيْن تنَيْن بيصير بَيْن ألفَيْن : السِرُ بَيْنَ إثْنَيْن يَصيرُ بَيْنَ ألفَيْن

A secret once shared by two is shared by a thousand.

Once you tell one person your secret, it is no longer a secret and others will hear.

سَلِّمْ سِرَّك لَلْناس بتِنْداس : إنْ سلَّمْتَ سرَّكَ للناسِ يدوسونَكَ

If you reveal your secret to people you will be crushed.

Learn to keep your secret rather than exposing yourself to others.

متل كَتاب مَفْتوحْ : مثلَ كتابٌ مفتوحٌ

Like an open book.

He is like an open book.

المَكْتوب مْبَيِّن من عِنْوانُه : المكتوبُ ظاهرٌ مِن عنوانِهِ

What is inside the book is clear from the cover.

To wear your heart on your sleeve.

صَدْرَك أوْسَع لِسِرَّك : صَدْرُك أوْسَعٌ لِسِرَّك

Your chest is wider than your secret.
(You have enough space for it in your chest. So don't give your secret away)

Keep your secret.

WEALTH

المال

المال ما بِيشتِري السعادِة : **المالُ لا يَشتَري السَعادةَ**

Money cannot buy happiness.

إلّة الرِزْأة رْيِحا : **قِلَّةُ الرِزْقَةِ راحَةٌ**

Having a small amount of money will mean fewer concerns.

Someone with less money has fewer concerns; money brings problems.

مال الحرام مِتل الماي المالحه ما بِيروي : **المالُ الحَرامُ مثلَ الماءِ المالِحةِ لا يَروي (مثل مصري بالأصِل)**

Stolen money is like salty water.

Stolen wealth does not satisfy.

عِنْدُه مَصاري ما بتاكِلا النار : **عندَهُ مالٌ لا تأكلُهُ النارُ**

He has so much money that fire cannot reach it.

He is very wealthy.

مال الحَرام ما بِيْدومْ : **مالُ الحَرامُ لا يَدومْ**

Stolen money does not last.

حُب المال أتّال : حُبُ المالِ قتَّالٌ

Love of money can kill you.

مال الخسيسْ لأُبْليسْ : مالُ الخسيسُ لأُبْليسِ

The evil person's money belongs to the devil.

مال الخَسيس بيروح فْطيسْ : مال الخَسيسُ لَيْسَ لَهُ قيمَة

The evil one's money rots away.

The evil one's money has no value.

الرزء السايِب بيعَلِّم الناس الحَرامْ : الرِزْقُ المَتْروكُ يُعَلِّمُ الناسَ السَرِقَةَ

Unprotected wealth will teach people theft.

Leaving your money and possessions unaccompanied will cause temptations and teach those who are otherwise honest to steal.

الصيت أفْضَل مِن الغِنى : الصيتُ أفضلُ مِنَ الغِنى

Reputation is better than wealth.

صيت غِنى ولا صيت فُئرْ : صيتْ غِنى وَلا صيتْ فُقِرْ

Reputation is wealth and lack of reputation is poverty.

It is enriching to have a good reputation and impoverishing to have a bad reputation.

خَيْر البر عاجِلَهُ : خَيْرُ البرِّ عاجِلَهُ (عَمل الخَيْر يجب أن يَتم بِسُرعة)

Charity comes in its quickness.

Someone who does charity should do it quickly and without talking about it.

PROBLEMS

المشاكل = الهم

مين راءب الناس مات هم : مَن راقَبَ النّاسَ ماتَ هَمَاً

Someone who is always surveying others will die filled with concern.

بيَعْمِل من الحَبي إبّي : يَعمَلُ مِنَ الحَبَّةِ قُبَّة

To make a pile out of a single seed.

To make a mountain out of a molehill.

الباب لّي بيجي مِنْه الريحْ سِدُّه وِسْتريحْ : البابُ الذي يأتي منهُ الريح سُدَهُ واستريح

Close the door from which a scent emanates. Then relax.

Avoid the place where you can feel there are problems.

إذا ما خِرْبِت ما بتُعْمَرْ : إنْ لَم تخْرُبْ لا تُعمَرْ

If something is not destroyed it cannot be rebuilt.

إذا ما كِبْرِت ما بتُزْغَر : إنْ لَم تكْبُرْ لا تصغُرْ

If it does not get big, then it will not get smaller.

If the problem does not grow larger, then you will not confront it in order to make it smaller.

النارُ ما بتدوبْ بالنارِ : النارُ لا تَذوبُ بالنارِ

Fire does not put out fire.

If you see someone upset, don't get too upset also or you will exasperate the problem.

ما تُصُبْ الزَيْت عالنارْ : لا تَصُبْ الزَيْتَ على النارِ

Don't pour oil on the fire.

Pouring oil on the fire is not the way to quench it.

لَي شاف مُصيبةٍ غَيْرُه بتْهونْ مُصيبتُه : مَنْ رأى مُصيبةً غَيْرِه هانتْ عَلَيْهِ مَصيبتُهُ

He who saw other people's problems forgets his own problems.

Someone else's problems were so great that they distracted him from his own problems.

مَن كتَم عِلَّتَهُ أتلَتْهُ : الذي يُخْبّئُ مشاكِلَهُ تُميتُهُ

He who hides his problems kills them.

He who hides his problems ends them.

زاد الطين بلّه : زادَ على الطينِ المَبْلولِ ماءً

To put more water on the clay.

To increase a person's problems

كيف ما زَتَّيْتو بيِجي واِقِف : كَيْفَما رمَيْتَهُ يأتي واقفاً

However you throw him, he comes out standing.

However much he gets embroiled in problems, he can take care of himself.

DEATH

الموت

المَوْت كاس عَكُل الناس : المَوْتُ كَأسٌ على كلِّ الناسِ

Death is a cup everyone will have.

Death will come to everyone.

لّي إلو مِدّي ما بتأتْلو شِدِّي : من لَهُ وَقتٌ لِيَعيشَ لا تَقْتُلُهُ الشدَّه

Someone who has time designated to his life will not die from harshness.

You won't die until it is your time no matter how hard your circumstances.

ألف أوْلِةٌ جَبان ولا أوْلِةٌ ألله يرْحَمُه : ألِف قَوْلِةٌ جَبان ولا قَوْلَةُ الله يرْحَمه

A thousand times a coward but not the utterance: "May God bless his soul."

Better to be called a coward than to be foolhardy and face death.

الخَسيسْ بيْروحْ فْطيس : الخَسيسُ يَموتُ فَطيسٌ

The evil man died letting off a rotten smell.

He was so evil that no one buried him.

مين خَلَّف ما ماتْ : مَن خَلَّفَ لَمْ يَمُتْ

Someone who procreates does not die.

ما حَداً بيْموتْ نائِصْ عُمر : لا أَحَدٌ يَموتُ ناقِصٌ عُمرَهُ

No one dies sooner than they were meant to.

المَوْت حَأٌ : المَوْتُ حَقٌّ

Death is a right.

When someone dies, people comfort those who are mourning saying that death is the right of the human being and all of us will face it.

GENERAL PROVERBS

متفرآت : متفرِّقات

الوِآيِه خَيْر مِن العِلاجْ : الوِقايةُ خَيْرٌ مِنَ العِلاجِ

Pay attention to your health so that you don't have to deal with getting cured later on.

An ounce of prevention is worth a pound of cure.

السكوت عَلامِة الرِضا : السكوتُ علامةُ الرضا

Silence is a sign of consent.

The individual did not answer, but this can be interpreted as a sign of consent.

الضحِك بِلا سَبَب مِن إلَّة الأدَبْ : الضحكُ بلا سببٍ مِنْ قلَّةِ الأدبِ

Laughing without reason is a sign of being impolite.

إِجِت الحَزينِه تِفْرَحْ ما لإِيِت إلا مَطْرَح : أتَتْ الحزينةُ لِتَفرحَ فَلَم تُلاقي لها مكان

The sad one wanted to feel joy but found no place for himself.

Whatever he does, he has no hope for happiness.

الأمانَه لازِم تِرجَعْ لأصْحابْها : الأمانةُ يجبُ أن تعودَ لأصحابِها

The trust should return to its owners.

That which is borrowed should be returned.

لَّي خْتَشو ماتو (مَثَل مَصري مُسْتَخْدَم في الشام) : الذينَ إخْتَشوا ماتوا

Those with shame died. (Based on an old Egyptian proverb referring to a fire that started in a public bath. All those who felt shame at showing their bare bodies remained in the public bath and died)

No one with honor is left.

الله يأدّم لّي في خَيْر : الله يُقَدِّمُ الذي فيهِ خَيْر

May God give that which is blessed to you.

ما تُوَصّي حَرِيص : لا توصي حريصاً

You don't need to give advice to the guard.

I am very, very careful. You don't need to ask me to exert caution.

يا غَريبْ كون أديب : يا غريب كُنْ أديب

Oh, Stranger, be polite.

When a person travels to another country he should be polite and accept the customs of the people.

بياخدنا عَالبَحر و بيرَجِّعْنا عُطْشانين : يأخُذُنا إلى البحرِ وَيُرجِعُنا عطشانين

He takes us to the sea and we return thirsty.

Referring to someone who is very cheap.

لِلضَرورَه أحْكامٌ : لِلضرورَةِ أحْكامٌ

Necessity has its own wisdom.

To be forced to do something out of necessity.

الحاجِه إم الإخْتِراغْ : الحاجةُ أُمُّ الإخْتِراعِ

Necessity is the mother of invention.

التاريخ بعيد نَفْسُه : التاريخُ يُعيدُ نفسَهُ

History repeats itself.

الغائِبْ حِجتُه معُه : الغائبُ حُجَّتَهُ مَعَهُ

A person who is absent has an excuse.

آخِر العِلاج الكَيْ : نهايةُ العلاجِ الكَيْ

The final cure is burning.

I'll be patient with him, but it is inevitable that in the end I will be hard on him.

ما على الرَسول إلا البلاغ : ليسَ على الرسولِ إلاَّ التبليغ

The messenger just relays the message.

فالِج ما تعالِج : فالِجٌ لا تُعالَج

A stroke has no cure.

A hopeless case

كل مَعْروض مَرْفوض وكُل ممنوع مَرْغوب : كُلُّ شَيْءٍ معروضٌ مَرفوضٌ وكلُّ شيْءٍ ممنوعٌ هو مرغوبٌ

All that is permitted is refused, and all that is prohibited is desired.

كل مَمْنوع مَرْغوب : كُلُّ ما هوَ ممنوعٌ مرغوبٌ

That which is prohibited is desired.

ما مات حأ ورا طالِب : ما ماتَ حَقٌّ وراءهُ طالِبٌ

A right that was asked for will not die.

If you ask for your rights you will get them.

نألَّب السِحِر عَالساحِر: انْقَلَبَ السِحِرُ عَلى الساحِرِ

The spell returned upon the person casting it.

Bad luck came back to the person who wished it upon another.

بُكْرا يْدوب التَلِج ويْبان المَرِج : غَداً يَذوبُ الثَلِجُ وَيظهَرُ المَرجُ (العشب الأخضر)

Tomorrow the snow will melt and grass will be seen.

Don't worry, the truth will soon be revealed.

لّي ضَرَبْ ضَرَب ولّي هَرَب هَرَبْ : الذي ضَرَبَ ضَرَبَ والذي هَرَبَ هَرَبْ

The person who hit, hit; the person who escaped, escaped.

Forget about it. It has happened and you can't do anything about it.

حتى تُطاع طلُبْ المسْتَطاعْ : لِكَيْ تُطاعْ أطْلُب المُسْتَطاع

In order to be obeyed, ask for what is possible.

الخَوْف من المُصيبي مصيبَة دايْمِه : الخَوْفُ مِنَ المُصيبَةِ مَصيبَةٌ دائِمَةٌ

Fear of a disaster is a perpetual disaster.

Fear of a disaster is a disaster in and of itself.

بُحْصَه بتِسْنُدْ خابِيِه : بُحصةٌ تَسْنُدُ خابِيَةً

A small pebble can support a large jar.

This refers to the importance of small things.

الصبرِ مِفْتاحْ الفَرَجْ : الصبرُ مُفتاحُ الفرجِ

Patience is the key to happiness.

البرِدْ والإلّي سبب كِل عِلّه : البَرْدُ وَالقِلَّةُ سَبَبُ كُلِ عِلَّةٍ

Cold and poverty cause all sickness.

شو نَفْع النَدَمْ بَعْدَ فَوات الأوانْ : ماذا يَنْفعُ الندمُ بعدَ فواتِ الوقتِ

What is the use of regret after time has passed?

There is nothing more you can do about this.

الوَلَد وَلَد ولَو حَكَم بَلَد : الولدُ ولدٌ حتى ولَوْ حكمَ بلداً

The young boy is a boy even if he rules a country.

كُبيرِ الأوْم خادِمْهُمْ : كَبيرُ القَوْمِ خادِمَهُمْ

The servant is the most important individual of the masses.

الحَأ يَعلو وَلا يُعْلى عَلَيْه : الحَقُ يَعلو وَلا يُعْلى عَلَيْهِ

Your rights are way up high and nothing is higher than them.

المَحَل المنيح مَحَل ما بتِسْتَريحْ : المكانُ الجيّدُ هوَ مكان حيثُ تَسْتَريحْ

A good place is a place where you can relax.

الحَرب بالنَظّارات هيِّن : الحَربُ مِن بَعيدٍ سَهِلٌ

Observing a war from far away is easy.

ما بيصِحْ إلاَّ الصَحيح : لَنْ يَحْدُثَ إلاَّ ما هو صحيحٌ (سليم)

Only good things will happen.

إن ماتت المروّة شو نَفع الأوّة : إن ما تتِ الشهامةُ ماذا تنفَعُ القُوَّةُ

If nobility can die then what good is strength.

المَعْيوب بيعِدْ لَلناس عْيوب : الذي فيهِ عَيْب يَرى عيوب الآخرين

He who is filled with faults sees the faults of others.

عذر ألأبَح من ذنِب : عذرٌ أقبَح مِن ذَنْبٍ

The apology is more stupid than the original error.

Don't make a mistake so you won't have to be in the position of apologizing and looking stupid.

خيْر الأمور الوَسَط : أفضَلُ الأمورِ في الوسَطِ (من دون المبالَغَة)

Good comes from the middle ground, not extremes.

خَيْر الأمور أوْسَطُها : خَيْرُ الأمورِ أوْسَطُها

The goodness of the events comes from the middle of it.

The good comes from the middle ground, not the extreme.

الجَمْرا ما بِتحرِقْ إلاّ مَحَلاّ : الجَمْرا لا تَحَرُقْ إلاّ مَكانِها

The coal only burns in one place.

When someone cannot empathize and feel someone else's pain.

لِّي ما بيخافْ مِن الله خافْ مِنْهُ : الذي لا يَخافُ مِن الله عَلَيْكَ أنْ تَخافَ مِنْهُ

Beware of he who does not fear God.

الزايِد خَيْ النائِص : الزائدُ مِثْلَ الناقِصِ

Abundance is the brother of shortage.

Don't be extreme. Take middle grounds. Neither extreme is good.

وَعد الحُر دَيْن : عندما يَعِدُ الحُر هذا دَيْنٌ عَلَيْهِ

The free man's promise is a debt that has to be paid.

When a man is free and promises something then he is responsible for that promise.

كلام الليْل بيِمحيه النّهار : كلامُ الليْلِ يَمْحوهُ النَهارُ

That which was spoken at night is erased in the day.

This has both positive and negative connotations. This proverb can mean that it is not good to keep a grudge, that something once spoken then can be forgotten. Or it can be that someone made a promise, but then broke it and said that the promise was given previously but not now.

رِجْعِت حَليمي لعادِتْها الأديمي : رَجِعَتْ حَليمةٌ لعادَتِها القَديمة

Halimeh returned to her old habits.

Describes someone who becomes her true self again.

الحَسود لا يَسود : الحَسودُ لا يَسودْ

The jealous person does not become important.

شوَّفُه نْجوم الضُّهر : أراهُ نُجومَ الظهرِ

Make him see the stars in the middle of the day.

Addresses someone who is very oppressed and tortured. A Syrian film was named after this expression. Sometimes if someone is hit, they imagine seeing stars in broad daylight.

يا ما تَحتَ السواهي دَواهي : بعضَ الأحيانِ هناكَ خَلْفَ الغباءِ ذكاء

Under his stupidity is hidden cleverness.

Crazy like a fox.

ترى الفِتيان كَالنَخل وما أدراكَ ما الدخل : ترى الفتيانَ كالنَخلِ وما أدراكَ ما في الداخلِ

Youth looks like a palm tree on outside but you don't know what is inside.

You don't know how it appears on the inside even though it is lovely on the outside.

حَسَبْنا الباشا باشا طُلع الباشا زلْمي : ظنَّينا أن الباشا هو باشا فإذا هو رَجُلٌ عاديٌّ

We thought he was a pasha and he turned out to be a regular man.

Used when someone turns out to be less important than originally thought.

شِفْناك فَوْء وْشِفْناك تَحِت = رأيْناكَ من فَوْق وَرَأيْناكَ من تَحِت (لآ أمل منكَ)
أين الثريّا من الثرى : أين النجمَة من الأرضِ

Where are the stars from the ground?

Comparing two different things

رضينا بالهمّ والهمّ ما رضي فينا : قَبِلْنا بأمرٍ تافهٍ ومع ذلِكَ لَم نحْصَلْ عَلَيْهِ

We accepted an insignificant outcome, but we didn't even accomplish that.

كرامَة الورد يُشرَب العِلَّيْء : كَرامَةُ الوردِ يَشرَبُ العُلَّيْقُ

Because of the flower, the bush is able to drink.

Someone benefiting from someone else's efforts (in the negative sense).

احسُبْ حْسابَك وارْكَبْ ركابَك : أُحْسُبْ حِسابَكْ واركَبْ رِكابَكْ

Calculate well at the beginning and then you can run off comfortably with the outcome.

Measure twice and cut once.

لَّي ما إلو كبير ما إلو تَدبير : الذي لَيْسَ لَهُ كَبير لَيْسَ عِنْدَهُ تَدْبير

Someone who does not have an elderly person to guide him has no one to train him.

الصباح رَباحْ : الصباحُ رَباحٌ

Morning is profit.

Let's wait until the next morning to deal with this. Not now.

اخْتَلَطَ الحابِلْ بالنابِلْ : إخْتَلَطَ الحابِلُ بِالنابِلِ

The trap got mixed with the shooting arrow

Chaos

الإنسانْ بيفَكِّر والرب بيدبِّر : الإِنْسانُ يُفَكِّرُ والرَبُ يُدَبِّرُ

The individual thinks and God will help him.

وَجَعْ ساعة وَلا كِل ساعة : أَلَمُ ساعة ولا أَلَمُ كُل ساعَة

Pain for an hour is better than pain for many hours.

لَي بَدَّك تؤَضي مْضي ولِّي بَدَك تِرهْنه بيعُه : الذي تُريدُ أن تَقضيَه إعملْهُ والذي تُريدُ أنْ تَرْهَنَهُ بِعْهُ

That which you want to finish, do; that which you want to gamble, sell.

Don't procrastinate.

كِلْ إنْسان فيه ما يُرْمى بيه : كُل إنْسان فيهِ ما يُرمى بِهِ (كُلُ إنْسان فيهِ عيوب)

Every human has something you can throw at him.

Every human has faults.

مينْ خَيَّرَك حَيَّرَك : مَن خَيَّرَك حَيَّرَكَ

He who gives you a choice confuses you.

Choices make decisions more confusing.

إنْتَ فَصِّل ونِحْنا مِنِلْبُسْ : أنتَ فَصِّل ونَحنُ نَلْبَس

You sew and we will dress.

You give orders and we will listen.

إضحَك بتِضحَكَلَك الدِني : إضْحَكْ تَضْحَكْ لكَ الدُنيا

Laugh and the world with laugh with you.

Be happy and you will find everything around you happy and peaceful too.

كُل إناء يَنْضَحْ بِما فيه : كُلُ وعاء يُظْهِرُ ما فيهِ

Every vessel flows with that which comes out of it.

If someone is good, they do good things; if someone is evil, they do evil things.

لا تَهرِفْ بِما لا تَعْرِف : لا تَمدَحْ ما لا تَعْرِفْهُ

Don't praise that which you do not know.

لَّي ما عِنْدُه كُبير بِشتري كُبير : مَن ليْسَ عِنْدَهُ شَخصٌ مُسِنٌ فَلْيَأتِي بِواحَدٍ

He who does not have elders, must buy an elderly person.

This proverb is about the importance of elders in one's life.

من الحَبِه بِتِنْبُت الشَجَرَة : مِنَ الحَبَّةِ تَنْبُتُ الشَّجَرَةُ

From a grain can grow a tree.

From something little, big important things can come. Everything – even small things – have a role in life.

المجنون بِيحكي والعائل بِيسْمَعْ : المَجنونُ يَحْكي والعاقِلْ يَسمعُ

The crazy one speaks and the rational one listens.

Even if you hear something not in your taste, better to be quiet and listen than to talk.

درْهم وآيِه خَيْر مِن أنطار عِلاجْ : دِرهَمُ وِقايةٌ خيرٌ مِن قِنْطارِ عِلاجّ

Be careful with your Dirham (old coin in the Levant). Better than to have to deal with getting cured.

Be careful of little things in your health before they become big problems.

173

ألِف مَرّة جَبان ولا مرّة أَلله يرحمُه : أَلفُ مَرَّة جَبانٌ ولا مرة أَلله يرحمَهُ

A thousand times a coward and not one time: "May God bless his soul."

Better to be very careful and even cowardly than to risk death.

شحَّاد ومْشارِطْ؟ : شَحادٌ وَمُشارِطٌ؟

A beggar with conditions.

This proverb describes someone asking for help, but with certain conditions.

كِل شي مِتِل ما بِيجي بيْروح : كُلُ شَيْء كما يَأتي يَذهَبُ

Everything that comes goes.

Easy comes, easy goes.

الحِفرة لّي بتُحفُرا لَغَيْرَك بتوعَ فيها : الحفرةُ التي تحْفِرُها لغَيْرِكَ تَقَعُ فيها

Only you will fall into the hole that you dig for others.

What comes around goes around.

آمِتْ الحَزينه تِفْرَح ما لئَتْ مَطْرَحْ : قامَتْ الحَزينَة لِتَفْرَح فَلَمْ تَجِد مكان

The sad one tried to be happy but found no place.

Refers to a really sad and pessimistic individual.

عِنْد العَزايِم أنْطونْ نايِم = عِنْدَ المناسَبات التي تتطَلَّب تَعَب أنْطون نائمٌ

During the festivities, Antoine was asleep.

Refers to a lazy person who is not helping at the time he is needed.

ما بِتْمنّاه حتى لَعَدوّي : لا أتمنّاهُ حتّى لِعَدوّي

Something that I do not wish even upon my enemies

بيروحْ على البَحرِ بينَشْفُه : يَذهَبُ الى البَحرِ فيَنَشِّفَهُ

He goes to the sea and dries it up.

He brings bad luck to those around him.

إسمَعِ وْكِب بالبَحرِ : إسمَعْ وارمي في البحرِ

Listen and throw into the sea.

In one ear and out the other ear. Don't take this too seriously.

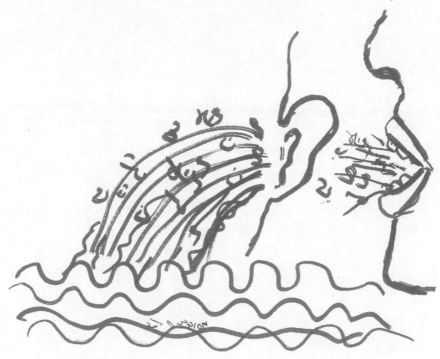

Rebecca Joubin is Malcolm O. Partin assistant professor and chair of Arab studies at Davidson College. She received her PhD from Columbia University in 2004. Before joining Davidson as in 2009, she conducted research in Syria for close to a decade. Some of this research is included in her most recent manuscript: *The Politics of Love: Sexuality, Gender, and Marriage in Syrian Television Drama* (2013). She has translated Moniru Ravanipur's *Afsaneh* (2013), and her articles in English and Arabic have been published in the *International Journal of Middle Eastern Studies, Middle East Journal, Arab Studies Journal, MERIP, al-Kifa al-Arabi,* and *al-Mada.* Her upper level Arab studies courses center around the politics of gender in Syrian art, culture, and media.

Etab Hreib is a critically acclaimed Syrian watercolorist from Der-Ez-Zor, who graduated from the Graphics Art Department of the University of Damascus. Since then, she has exhibited her work in Algeria, Egypt, Syria, Lebanon, Iraq, Jordan, Morocco, Tunisia, China, Bulgaria, France, Spain, Germany, and the United States. She was the recipient of the al-Mahros Award in Tunisia, a Golden Award from the Ministry of Culture in China, and an award for best Arab artist from the Ministry of Culture in Algeria. In addition to working full time as an artist, she has taught at the Fine Arts Department at Damascus University, has given painting courses for diabetic children, has taught ceramics to blind children, and has worked as a set and costume designer for Syrian theater, film, and television drama. She also served as a juror for the Adonis Prize for Best TV series.